I0643809

AMERICA'S STORY

Historical Sources on the Great Depression

CHET'LA SEBREE AND ADRIANE RUGGIERO

Cavendish Square
New York

Published in 2020 by Cavendish Square Publishing, LLC
243 5th Avenue, Suite 136, New York, NY 10016

First Edition

Library of Congress Cataloging-in-Publication Data

Names: Sebree, Chet'la, author. | Ruggiero, Adriane, author.
Title: Historical Sources on the Great Depression / Chet'la Sebree and Adriane Ruggiero.
Description: First edition. | New York : Cavendish Square, 2020. |
Series: America's story | Includes bibliographical references and index.
Identifiers: LCCN 2018033081 (print) | LCCN 2018039367 (ebook) |
ISBN 9781502640970 (ebook) | ISBN 9781502640963 (library bound) | ISBN 9781502640956 (pbk.)
Subjects: LCSH: United States--History--1933-1945--Sources--Juvenile literature. |
United States--History--1919-1933--Sources--Juvenile literature. |
New Deal, 1933-1939--Sources--Juvenile literature. |
Depressions--1929--United States--Sources--Juvenile literature.
Classification: LCC E806 (ebook) | LCC E806 .S43 2019 (print) | DDC 973.916--dc23
LC record available at https://lccn.loc.gov/2018033081

Editorial Director: David McNamara
Copy Editor: Nathan Heidelberger
Associate Art Director: Alan Sliwinski
Designer: Christina Shults
Production Coordinator: Karol Szymczuk
Photo Research: J8 Media

The photographs in this book are used by permission and through the courtesy of: Cover, General Photographic Agency/Getty Images, (background and used throughout) Foxstudio/Shutterstock.com; p. 4 John Carnemolla/Corbis/Getty Images; p. 7 FPG/Hulton Archive/Getty Images; p. 9, 102 Dorothea Lange/Library of Congress; p. 25 Ben Shahn/Library of Congress; p. 45 Library of Congress; p. 62 Jet Lowe/Library of Congress; p. 116 Howard R. Hollem/Library of Congress; p. 122 Lester Beall/Library of Congress; p. 10 Underwood Archives/Getty Images; p. 16 Congress/Corbis/VCG/Getty Images; p. 18, 47, 58 Corbis/Getty Images; p. 20 Library of Congress/Wikimedia Commons/File:Littered floor of Stock Exchange after market session, New York City LCCN94509160.jpg/Public Domain; p. 27, 39, 40, 49, 73, 84, 114 Bettmann/Getty Images; p. 30 Chicago History Museum/Getty Images; p. 34 Walter B. Lane/The LIFE Picture Collection/Getty Images; p. 37 MPI/Getty Images; p. 54, 86 Universal History Archive/Getty Images; p. 66, 90 Fotosearch/Archive Photos/Getty Images; p. 95 John Chillingworth/Picture Post/Getty Images; p. 88, 128-129 Ullstein Bild/Getty Images.

Printed in the United States of America

AMERICA'S STORY

CONTENTS

Photographs are primary sources. In this photo, people wait in unemployment lines. These people were seeking either work or financial assistance during the Great Depression.

Primary Sources

In the pages that follow, you will hear from many different people from a time in America's past. These selections will vary in length. Some are long, and others are short. You'll find many easy to understand at first reading, but some may require several readings. All the selections have one thing in common, however. They are primary sources. They are important to us because they are the core material for all historical investigation.

What Is a Primary Source?

The term "primary source" is the name historians give to the information that makes up the record of human existence. A primary source is "history" itself. Primary sources are evidence. They give historians the all-important clues they need to understand the past.

Perhaps you have read a detective story in which an investigator has to solve a mystery by piecing together bits of evidence that he or she uncovers. The detective makes deductions, or educated guesses based on the evidence, and solves the mystery once all the deductions point in a certain direction. Historians work in much the same way. Like detectives, they analyze data through careful reading and rereading. After much analysis, they draw conclusions about an event, a person, or an entire era. Different historians may analyze the same evidence and come to different conclusions. That is why there is often strong disagreement about an event.

Primary sources are also called documents. It is a rather dry word to describe what can be just about anything: an official speech by a government leader, an old map, an act of Congress, a letter, a diary entry, a newspaper article, a song, a poster, a cartoon, a photograph, or someone captured on tape or film.

By examining the following primary sources, you will be taking on the role of historian. Here is a chance to jump into an intense period in US history: the Great Depression. You'll come to know the voices of the men and women who lived during those years when Americans experienced poverty, hunger, and hopelessness. You'll read the letters they wrote to their president and the diary entries they penned—the words they used to express their thoughts about what was happening around them.

How to Read a Primary Source

Each document in this book deals with the Great Depression and America's reaction to that tense time in its history. Some of the documents are from government publications. Others are from the official papers of President Franklin D. Roosevelt and the men and women in his administration. Many of the documents are letters written by ordinary people asking for help to buy food, to pay debts, and to survive. All of the documents, major and minor, help us to understand what it was like to live during the Great Depression.

BROOKLYN DAILY EAGLE

And Complete Long Island News

LATE NEWS

WALL STREET 1:15 PRICES

89th YEAR—No. 295. NEW YORK CITY, THURSDAY, OCTOBER 24, 1929. 32 PAGES THREE CENTS

WALL ST. IN PANIC AS STOCKS CRASH

Attempt Made to Kill Italy's Crown Prince

ASSASSIN CAUGHT IN BRUSSELS MOB; PRINCE UNHURT

Royal Suitor Was About to Lay Wreath on Unknown Soldiers' Tomb.

Princess, Deeply Moved, Falls Into Fiance's Arms and Kisses Him

Hollywood Fire Destroys Films Worth Millions

ATTEMPT MADE ON LIFE

Crown Prince Humbert.

Consolidated Studios Are Swept by Flames Fatal to One—Master Pictures Burned Include Many New Talkie Productions.

FEAR 52 PERISHED IN LAKE MICHIGAN; FERRY IS MISSING

Wreckage Picked Up Indicates Craft Went Down With All Aboard.

PIECE OF PLANE LIKE DITEMAN'S IS FOUND AT SEA

Black and Orange Wreckage Indicates Daring Flier Went to Death.

High Duty Group Gave $700,000 to Coolidge Drive

Grundy Agrees Rates Went Up Due to His Activities as Propagandist. Favors More Lobbying to 'Carry Out Voters' Wish.'

FOR MORE LOBBYISTS

JOSEPH R. GRUNDY

STOCKS CRASH IN RUSH TO SELL; BILLIONS LOST

Morgan, Mitchell Buying Stocks in Effort to Check Rush to Unload.

CARNEGIE CHARGE OF PAID ATHLETES ROUSES COLLEGES

HOOVER'S TRAIN HALTED BY AUTO PLACED ON RAILS

WARDER SOUGHT TO KEEP SEA TRIP SECRET, AID SAYS

SOMERS NAMED AS HEAD OF NEW EXCHANGE BANK

Primary sources like newspapers provide us with information about what people were thinking, feeling, and doing during a certain moment in history. Although many people thought the stock market crash of 1929 caused the Great Depression, it was just one of the many elements of the financial crisis.

The selections you will read may be difficult to understand at first. There will be a variety of styles, from very formal to quite informal. Don't let the writing put you off. Interpreting these kinds of documents is exactly the sort of work a historian does.

As you read each document, ask yourself some basic questions. Who is writing or speaking? Who is that person's intended audience? What is he or she trying to tell the audience? Is the message clearly expressed or is it implied, or stated indirectly? What words does the writer use to convey his or her message? Are the words emotional or neutral in tone? These are questions that can help you think critically about a primary source.

There are also some tools in each chapter to help you unpack these documents. Some terms and concepts you may not be familiar with have been explained in sidebars. Also, questions follow each of the documents to help you focus and think through the primary source you have just read. As you read each selection, you'll probably come up with many questions of your own. That's great! The work of a historian always leads to many, many questions. Some can be answered, while others will require more investigation.

Even formerly wealthy plantation owners in the South felt the sting of the Depression. This primary source depicts a formerly enslaved couple sitting on the steps of a plantation house falling into ruins in the 1930s.

Although there were some conservative movements, the United States experienced great economic growth and social change, like women gaining the right to vote and enjoying more freedoms, in the 1920s.

INTRODUCTION

A Decade of Financial Crisis

The Great Depression was a period of economic hardship in the United States that lasted from 1929 until around 1939. The economy is the way a nation's goods and services are produced, distributed, and used. During the 1930s, the financial crisis brought the economy of the United States to a near standstill, caused hardship and suffering for millions, and affected nations throughout the world. What made the Depression's impact so powerful was the fact that it followed a period of relative wealth and hopefulness in the United States: the Roaring Twenties. That era came to an abrupt end when the stock market crashed in 1929.

The Roaring Twenties

The time period before the Great Depression in the United States was a time of invention, social change, and economic expansion that had begun in the years following

World War I (1914–1918). It was an age of sweeping changes. For the first time, more Americans lived in cities than on farms or in rural areas. Similarly, many African Americans moved north during the Great Migration to escape some of the racial tension in the South. In addition to changes in where people lived, there were great changes to how people lived. In the 1920s, people saw the invention of things like the traffic light and the radio.

The 1920s also brought about a time in which people were scared of communism, a political system in which the government owns and controls everything, and everything is to be equally shared among the country's people. Similarly, people were largely against immigration, or people from other countries moving to the United States in hopes of making it their permanent residence. Some feared that new immigrants were taking away jobs from people whose families immigrated decades earlier. In 1924, Congress passed the Johnson-Reed Act, which limited the number of immigrants who could come to the United States. Overall, in the 1920s, there was a great fear that outsiders would damage the tight-knit fabric of American culture, which was doing quite well.

During this period, wealth also seemed to skyrocket. With wealth came consumer culture. People purchased clothes, appliances, and cars for the first time. Additionally, women gained a new place in society during the 1920s. The Nineteenth Amendment, passed in 1920, gave women the right to vote in national elections for the first time in US history. On the heels of that amendment, women enjoyed many more freedoms in society. Some of these women, with their newfound freedoms, were often called flappers, wearing shorter hairstyles and less form-fitting clothing.

In general, many Americans had achieved a comfortable life in the 1920s. They owned their homes and cars. They went on vacations and bought on credit, which meant people bought things with the promise of paying for them later—like using a credit card rather than cash.

The Stock Market Boom

Additionally, some people were buying stock. A stock is a share in a company. A share is one of the equal parts of a company's capital, or money. People who own shares are entitled, or have a right, to a portion of the company's profits. As a company is more and more successful, the more and more the share prices increase. As the share prices increase, people who have purchased shares can sell off their shares to make a profit or purchase more shares in hopes of making an even bigger profit in the future.

Although most Americans did not own stock in 1929, there were many business opportunities for an eager investor, or someone who is willing to put money into the stock market in hopes of making money. There were whole businesses, such as trusts and holding companies, that existed for the sole purpose of investing in stocks.

Consumers were also able to buy shares of stock on margin. To buy things on margin meant that the consumer was putting only a little money down and owed the rest to the broker. Brokers, or people who buy and sell goods, assets, and stocks for other people, got the money to fund the loans from the nation's banks or major corporations. In other words, there were a number of people and businesses involved in the stock market.

During the 1920s, there were also few controls over the stock market. For that reason, investors believed that stock prices would go higher and higher, and they would get richer and richer. For a time, this is exactly how the stock market worked.

The Crash and the Depression

As will be explained more in chapter 1, eventually this time of rapid wealth and growth came to an end. In October 1929, people started rapidly selling off shares of stock. The rapid selling off of shares quickly reduced the prices of them, which caused the stock market crash on October 29, 1929. It is a day that has gone down in history as the Great Crash of 1929, or Black Tuesday. For a long time, people believed that this stock market crash caused the Great Depression.

Historians now agree that the Great Crash itself did not cause the Depression, as the loss of wealth was actually relatively small. However, the crash's psychological, or mental and emotional, effect was huge. Americans looked to the nation's banking and business leaders for answers to what caused the financial crisis, but none came. They looked to President Herbert Hoover for help when businesses closed their doors and workers were laid off. His promise that "prosperity is just around the corner" rang false when the economy failed to recover.

The Depression reached its depths in 1933, when approximately one-fourth of Americans were jobless. This unemployment rate did not begin to ease until 1939, when World War II broke out in Europe. In response to the war, American industries and workers began to produce planes, ships, and weapons for the nation's allies. America's participation in the war, beginning in 1941, finally helped to lift the country out of the Depression as all attention shifted to the task of fighting and winning a global war.

The Causes

Historians and economists continue to debate the reasons for the Great Depression. They point to easy credit and buying on credit. They point to the unequal division of wealth between American workers and business owners. They point to an excess of profits in the hands of industry. They also consider the overproduction of farm produce and consumer goods and the underconsumption, or limited purchase, of these products by the public. Additionally, they think the weakness of labor unions, or organizations of workers formed to protect their rights and interests at a company, may have had an effect. They believe all of these factors had just as much an effect on the Great Depression as overspeculation, or the assumption that stocks would make more of a profit than they actually could. Whatever the cause was, the Great Depression had an incredible impact.

The Impact

Economists and political leaders expect economies to go through periods of growth, slowdowns, and recovery. However, the Depression of the 1930s was more severe and lasted longer than any other in US history. During the Depression, there was a dramatic shift in people's beliefs about the strength of the nation's economy. The public's lack of confidence contributed to the length of the crisis, in which prices fell; industrial production slowed down; individuals and businesses went bankrupt, or legally declared that they could not pay their debts; and workers lost their jobs. The economy did not fix itself after a few years as business and government leaders had hoped. Instead, it continued its downward spiral. The effects of the decline touched nearly all segments of society and forced Americans to question their economic and political system as never before.

FDR and the New Deal

The story of the Great Depression cannot be separated from the presidency of Franklin Delano Roosevelt, who is often called simply by his initials, FDR. He defeated President Hoover in the election of 1932. FDR would go on to lead the United States for a record-breaking twelve years.

During these years, he would craft the New Deal, the name given to his plan to pull America out of the Depression. The number of jobless Americans began to decline during FDR's first term in office (1933–1937), when a wide variety of emergency

Franklin Roosevelt was the longest-serving president in US history. He served three full terms, beginning in 1933, and part of a fourth term. He died in office in 1945.

government programs to relieve human suffering and stimulate the economy came into existence. Among these programs was the Civilian Conservation Corps (CCC), a work program for primarily young, unmarried men. They were given food, medical care, and a place to live while they worked to conserve, or take care of, natural landscapes. They did things like plant trees and maintain forest roads. Over the nine years of its existence, the CCC employed close to three million men. Similarly, the Public Works Administration employed people to build public buildings, like hospitals, schools, and courthouses, as well as highways and bridges. The New

Deal also brought about programs like the National Recovery Administration (NRA), which established certain workplace codes like the maximum hours a person could work in a week, and the Agricultural Adjustment Administration (AAA), which provided aid to farmers and revitalized the agricultural industry. There were many other programs, each known by its own set of initials, amusingly referred to as "alphabet soup." Programs of relief, or money, food, and clothing given to those in need, and recovery continued during Roosevelt's second term in office (1937–1941).

Many Americans applauded the New Deal legislation, or laws, and looked at Roosevelt as the man who saved them and the nation from ruin. Others were less positive. Some thought Roosevelt's spending on huge public projects was reckless. They feared placing so much power into the hands of the president. It reminded some people of communism, in which the government has a lot of control. Others felt that Roosevelt and the New Deal did not go far enough to correct the issues with society and the economy. Hardly anyone who grew up during the Depression was a neutral observer of the events taking place. For too many Americans, it was a time of fear, poverty, and insecurity. For others, especially those involved in government, it was an exciting time when new ideas and approaches to solving problems were put into action.

Public Programs and "Big Government"

The Depression of the 1930s saw major changes in the relationship between the government and the American people. During the New Deal, the federal government took an active role in the nation's economy. It developed hydroelectric, or water-powered, projects in rural areas, established guidelines and codes for businesses, created jobs, and trained workers. This did not happen without controversy, however. Many people opposed the invasion of government into the way business was conducted and disliked its attempt to control the economy. They called this "big government."

Men in the Civilian Conservation Corps lived in military-like conditions in camps. Here, they are standing for morning line-up before work.

Most Americans, however, were grateful for the government's efforts to provide security and help for the elderly, the impoverished, and the disabled. The creation of a national system of social security is one of the most outstanding results of the New Deal legislation. To this day, this federal program provides benefits to people who are retired, unemployed, or disabled. The Roosevelt administration also made vast improvements to the nation's infrastructure, or public buildings and facilities. Many of the bridges, highways, national parks, schools, libraries, post offices, and courthouses Americans enjoy today were built by people working for New Deal programs.

Stories from This Era

Despite the ways in which Roosevelt was able to help the country recover from the economic crisis, the Great Depression was an incredibly difficult period in US history. Poverty, hunger, and fear cast a dark shadow over the country. The stories from this era tell of shock and despair but also of hope and courage.

The floor of the New York Stock Exchange (pictured here) would be littered with paper tickets used to write down prices and quantities of stocks after a day of trading.

1 *The Shock*

On September 3, 1929, the prices of shares of stock reached record-setting highs. Shares in such established companies as General Electric, American Telephone and Telegraph, and US Steel soared to new heights: $396, $304, and $262 per share, respectively. To give you some context about how much that would have been, a dollar in 1929 would be equivalent to more than $14.50 in 2018. So, for instance, the shares listed above would be worth about $5,800, $4,500, and $3,800 in 2018. This would have been the price for a single share, and most people owned more than a single share in a company.

The Leaking Bubble

The bubble that had been inflated by rapidly rising stock prices began to lose air, slowly at first, after this record high. Later in September, prices began to drop. Most investors were not concerned, however. As mentioned before, the stock market on which shares are traded, or purchased and sold, naturally goes up and down. For that reason, people who owned stock continued to hold their stock. They believed the market would recover, and it did. Investors looked forward to greater profits and the opportunity to buy even more shares. It seemed to them, on paper at least, that it was so easy to get rich.

Then, in October, the decline truly began again. Investors started to take notice. On October 23, many investors frantically began to sell off their stocks. Much of the value gained in previous months was lost in the morning's trading. Panic followed. Stockbrokers were flooded with calls from their clients to SELL! SELL! SELL! Clients wanted to get whatever money they could as share prices fell.

On Thursday, October 24, investors began a feverish sell-off again. Despite statements of confidence issued by the nation's leading bankers, the market could not be steadied. On Tuesday, October 29 (later called Black Tuesday), the bubble finally burst. Stockbrokers gave up all hope of recovering the previous days' losses. The downward movement of the stock market continued through the middle of November, when about $25 billion in investments had been lost. In 2018, that would have been close to $370 billion. It was the biggest market collapse in US history.

The crash marked the end of the Roaring Twenties. Hopes of prosperity were dashed, and gloom set in across the country.

A Stockbroker Remembers the Crash

Many people had placed their life savings in the stock market. They lost everything in the crash. John Hersch was a Chicago stockbroker and investor in 1929. Part of his job included keeping the figures on individuals who were carrying stocks on margin. In addition to his clients losing money, Hersch also lost most of his savings in the crash. The following is his description of how the crash ultimately ended up happening.

> The Crash—it didn't happen in one day. There were a great many warnings. The country was crazy ... It was a mad dream of get-rich-quick.
>
> You had no governmental control of margins, so people could buy on a shoestring. And when they began pulling the plug ... you had a deluge of weakness. You also had short-selling and a lack of rules.
>
> Anything went, and everything did go.
>
> —From Studs Terkel, *Hard Times: An Oral History of the Great Depression* (New York: The Free Press, 1986).

CONSIDER THIS

1. In Hersch's opinion, what caused the collapse of the stock market?
2. Hersch lost his savings in the collapse. Do you think he lost his job? What do you think he did to survive after the crash?

KEY TERMS AND CONCEPTS

From John Hersch's account:

deluge A flood.

margin Margin account, or a broker's account which allows investors to purchase stocks and bonds with borrowed money. These accounts require assets, such as a house or car, as collateral. In other words, the house or the car would be given up if investors could not pay back the borrowed money.

short-sell To sell stocks without having them in one's possession at the time of the sale; the seller hopes that when it comes time to deliver the shares, the price of the stock will have gone down and he can buy it again at a lower price, thus making money.

From Gordon Parks's account:

laid off Fired from a job.

personnel Employees.

Coming of Age During the Depression

By 1930, hundreds of businesses were closing and laying off their workers. Banks began to fail after customers rushed to withdraw their cash. The December 1930 closing of the Bank of the United States in New York City was one of the most notable failures. In one day, thousands of people collectively withdrew $2 million from the bank. The bank closings took away the life savings of ordinary men and women, who had come to view the financial institutions as safe places for their hard-earned dollars.

This was not uncommon, and it was even more common for this not to just happen to big businesses but to families. For instance, Diana Morgan was from a wealthy family who owned

The Great Depression affected all aspects of life. People losing their jobs meant they weren't able to put food on the table or roofs over their families' heads.

a general store in North Carolina. When the Depression hit, the store's customers, who were local farmers and townspeople, lost their farms and jobs. They could no longer afford to shop at the general store. Eventually, Morgan's family lost the store and went bankrupt.

However, for just as many Americans, the stock market crash of 1929 had little or no meaning. They owned no shares, had little or no savings, and were used to scraping by as farmers and laborers. These were the "old poor." For them, the Depression just meant more of the same. Some, however, did have hopes and plans for the future. Among them was a young African American named Gordon Parks. For him, the crash meant a sudden and rude detour.

In the following selection, Parks recalls the events of 1929. He was born in Fort Scott, Kansas, in 1912 and left home at age sixteen to live with his sister in Saint Paul, Minnesota. For a while, he worked part-time as a bellboy in an exclusive club for the city's wealthy businessmen. Gordon Parks eventually became a world-famous photographer, filmmaker, writer, and poet.

> On the fifteenth of October, I asked Sally if she would marry me. She ... explained, "Why ... I must finish high school ..." Common sense warned me to finish high school too ... I opened a savings account, anticipating the day ... when we would both graduate.
>
> The employees' locker room at the club was unusually quiet when I arrived at work one Wednesday that same month ... The cause for silence was tacked to the bulletin board. It read: "... some personnel will be laid off the first of next month ..."
>
> By Thursday the entire world knew ... I couldn't imagine such financial disaster touching my small world ... But by the first week of November I too

Men would swarm these San Francisco docks in hopes of a day's worth of work during the Depression.

KEY TERMS AND CONCEPTS

From Ed Paulsen's account:

hole An area inside of a cargo ship where raw goods are stored.

Pinkerton cops Security men hired by the company.

knew differently; ... I was without a job. ... On the seventh of November I went to school and cleaned out my locker ...

—From Gordon Parks, *A Choice of Weapons* (New York: Harper & Row, 1965).

CONSIDER THIS

1. What did Parks do to plan for the future?
2. In what other ways do you think the crash affected Parks? What do you think he did after he left school?

Down at the Docks

As businesses closed and employees were laid off, more and more workers competed for fewer and fewer jobs. Men even left their homes and families to search for work.

In the following excerpt, Ed Paulsen recalls what it was like being a recent high school graduate in 1930. He left his South Dakota home and traveled through the West doing odd jobs. After a few months, he found himself in San Francisco looking for work on the docks. In the excerpt below, he describes the "shape up" at the docks. During a shape up, a company foreman, or supervisor, selects workers for the day from a group of men eager to get noticed and be given work.

> I'd get up at five in the morning and head for the waterfront. Outside the Spreckles Sugar Refinery ... there would be a thousand men. You know dang well there's only three or four jobs. The guy [hiring boss] would come out with two little Pinkerton cops: "I need two guys ... to go into the hole." A thousand men would fight like ... dogs to get through there.
>
> —From Studs Terkel, *Hard Times: An Oral History of the Great Depression* (New York: The Free Press, 1986).

CONSIDER THIS

1. What do you think the men who did not get selected did with the rest of their days?
2. Do you think the three or four men who were selected to work on one day were guaranteed work the next day?

In Search of Aid

As the shock subsided, or calmed, people settled in for a long decade of uncertainty. Many looked to the government, and specifically the president, for guidance and aid.

Herbert Hoover had only been president for a few months when the stock market crashed in October 1929.

2

The Failure of Rugged Individualism

There were two different presidents during the Depression: Herbert Hoover and Franklin Delano Roosevelt. They took dramatically different approaches to the financial crisis. Hoover believed in rugged individualism. This was the concept that each person should be able to take care of himself or herself without any help from the government. Roosevelt took a wildly different approach. He developed a series of public programs and job opportunities in hopes of helping the economy bounce back. People had a variety of responses to both approaches.

Hoover's State of the Union Address

On December 3, 1929, President Hoover addressed Congress in his annual State of the Union message. Herbert Hoover came to the presidency on the Republican ticket in 1928 after gaining fame for his humanitarian work, or work focused on the well-being of others, during and after World War I. He was a skilled leader and cared deeply about human suffering.

Before becoming president, Hoover had been the secretary of commerce (1921–1928). In this role, he was responsible for promoting US businesses and industries while also developing foreign and domestic trade relationships. For that reason, it would make sense for him to be able to help the economy recover.

Hoover optimistically believed that the Depression was only a temporary emergency. The following account is how he explained the stock market crash and its impact.

> The country has enjoyed a large degree of prosperity and sound progress during the past year ... The long upward trend of fundamental progress, however, gave rise to over-optimism as to profits, which translated itself into a wave of uncontrolled speculation in securities, resulting in the diversion of capital from business to the stock market and the inevitable crash. The natural consequences have been a reduction in the consumption of luxuries and semi-necessities by those who have met with losses, and a number of persons thrown temporarily out of employment.
>
> —From President Herbert Hoover's First Annual State of the Union message, December 3, 1929. In Fred L. Israel, ed., *The State of the Union Messages of the Presidents, 1905–1966* (New York: Chelsea House, 1966).

KEY TERMS AND CONCEPTS

From President Herbert Hoover's State of the Union address:

securities Stocks and bonds.

CONSIDER THIS

1. According to the president, how did "over-optimism" about potential profits lead to the crash?
2. What might Hoover have meant by "fundamental progress"?
3. Would you have been alarmed if you had heard the president's speech?

Senator La Follette Jr. Blames Hoover

Robert M. La Follette Jr., a US senator from Wisconsin, wrote the following article for the *Nation* magazine in 1931. He attacks the Hoover administration and its philosophy of "rugged individualism," words Hoover used in a 1928 campaign speech. According to Hoover, the success of the American system was based on the concepts of ordered liberty, equal opportunity, self-reliance, and individual initiative. Hoover, like many other Americans, felt the government should stay outside the lives of citizens. La Follette Jr. clearly did not agree.

Robert M. La Follette Jr., shown here, followed in the footsteps of his father, Robert Sr., as a US senator from Wisconsin. Both men were known for their progressive political ideas.

> Unemployment has been spreading poverty and … suffering … No one yet knows when the present economic disaster will … end … Responsibility for the failure … to provide … relief … rests squarely upon President Hoover. The bankruptcy of his leadership … reveals the tragic failure of rugged individualism.
>
> —From the *Nation*, July 15, 1931.

CONSIDER THIS

1. How would you describe La Follette's tone in this article?
2. Why do you think the senator believed the philosophy of "rugged individualism" was a failure?

One Man's Plea

President Hoover was very opposed to "big government." He felt that it was not the role of the federal government to become involved in providing relief to those hurt by the Depression. That responsibility, he thought, lay with local governments and privately funded charities. To help revive the economy, he urged businesses to hire workers and expand production. He also called on farmers to plant fewer crops to avoid flooding the market and pushing crop prices lower.

Despite his belief that people should help themselves, Hoover did establish a government agency to stimulate economic activity. In 1932, he created the Reconstruction Finance Corporation (RFC). The agency provided financial support to state governments, banks, businesses, and even average Americans. For instance, in 1932 alone, it loaned $1.5 billion to save banks and businesses. Hoover hoped that this money would help bring financial balance back to the country.

Despite Hoover's efforts, the economy fell into a steep, steady decline. People still could find no work, the poor got hungrier, and crop prices continued to drop. Many Americans believed Hoover and the government weren't doing enough to help them. The following letter was written to the president by an unemployed worker from Pottstown, Pennsylvania, in October 1930.

> I am persuaded to write you, concerning aid to unemployment ... It really is alarming that this so called prosperous nation ... must suffer [on account] of a few men seeking power and ... [seeking to] have laws [passed] to suit themselves ...
>
> —From Robert S. McElvaine, ed., *Down and Out in the Great Depression: Letters from the Forgotten Man* (Chapel Hill, NC: University of North Carolina Press, 1983).

CONSIDER THIS

1. Whom does the writer blame for the crisis? Do you think he is correct to blame them?
2. What do you think he thought of Hoover?

Growing Unrest

It wasn't just a senator or a few individuals that were frustrated with Hoover. People who even served the government in the military grew increasingly frustrated with Hoover's approach to the financial crisis.

Unemployed men who had fought in World War I decided to march on Washington in 1932 to demand the payment of a bonus, or a sum of money given as a reward in addition to someone's salary, promised to them by the federal government. The bonus was not to be paid until 1945, but the veterans wanted—and needed—it immediately. They formed what came to be known as the Bonus Army.

In the summer of 1932, members of the Bonus Army converged, or came together, in Washington, DC. Other jobless men soon joined the group, many with their families. At the peak, there were about twelve thousand to fifteen thousand men and

While the Senate decided whether or not to give the World War I veterans their bonuses early, the frustrated marchers held a demonstration on the steps of the Capitol, where the Senate meets.

veterans, along with their wives and children, camped out in the outskirts of Washington.

President Hoover refused to meet with the bonus marchers or discuss their demands. He regarded them as hoodlums and political radicals intent on bringing about a revolution. In July, Hoover ordered the US Army to break up the group. It erupted in violence, and one marcher died.

A Desire for New Leadership

President Hoover told Americans to remain optimistic, and business leaders urged consumers to spend money to boost business and people's confidence in the economy. Yet Americans were unable to find work. Without money to buy food or pay rent, many became homeless. In rural areas, families took to living in tents, even in the winter. In open lots in and around cities, people lived in groups of wood and tin shacks that came to be known mockingly as Hoovervilles. The economic system appeared broken, and the nation's leadership appeared incapable of putting it back together. While some Americans blamed themselves for their misfortune, others blamed Herbert Hoover. As the Depression continued, people began to lose hope. It is not surprising that people were eager for a change during the 1932 election.

Hoovervilles popped up all across the United States during the Depression. For instance, this 1934 image is of a Hooverville in Seattle, Washington.

Before Roosevelt became president, or contracted polio for that matter, he ran as James A. Cox's running mate during Cox's unsuccessful 1920 presidential campaign.

3 A Change in Power

In the 1932 election, voters overwhelmingly rejected the idea of reelecting Hoover. Many felt he had done little to help pull the nation out of the economic crisis. Franklin Delano Roosevelt, who was then serving as the governor of New York, ran as the Democratic Party's candidate. He won the election. In his nomination acceptance speech, FDR promised to deliver a "new deal for the American people." What the new deal meant remained to be seen.

The Road to the Presidency

Roosevelt came from a wealthy New York family. He was a cousin of former president Theodore Roosevelt and was married to Theodore's niece Eleanor. Raised in upper-class surroundings on an estate in Hyde Park, Roosevelt chose to devote himself to politics.

His rise was rapid. He served first in the New York State Legislature, the state's lawmaking body. Then he served as assistant secretary of the navy. In 1920, he ran unsuccessfully as the vice-presidential candidate.

When he fell sick with polio in 1921, Roosevelt lost the use of his legs. However, the disease did not take any of his ambition and drive. He continued to pursue political office and was elected governor of New York in 1928. Four years later, he was elected president of the United States in the midst of the Great Depression.

Roosevelt had promised Americans that he would do something to solve the crisis, and he did. During his first one hundred days in office, Congress passed much of the legislation he requested. Collectively, the programs born of this legislation were called the New Deal.

The Reality of the Depression

Before he was elected president, Roosevelt made a point of commenting on the current financial situation. On May 22, 1932, presidential hopeful Franklin Delano Roosevelt was given an honorary degree by Oglethorpe University in Georgia. These types of degrees are given to important people and figures who did not actually attend the university. When given the degree, Roosevelt addressed the graduating class. In his speech, he demanded a radical response to the nation's economic crisis. An excerpt from his speech follows.

> The year 1928 does not seem far in the past, but since that time … the world about us has experienced significant changes. Four years ago … you could expect to take your place in a society well supplied with material things and could look forward to … living in your own homes, each … with a two-car garage; and, without great effort, would be providing

yourselves and your families with all the necessities and amenities of life.

How sadly different is the picture which we see around us today! If only the mirage [of prosperity] had vanished, we should not complain ... But with it have vanished, not only the easy gains of speculation, but much of the savings of thrifty and prudent men and women ... More calamitous still, there has vanished ... the certainty of today's bread and clothing.

You have been struck, I know, by the tragic irony of our economic situation today. We have not been brought to our present state by any natural calamity ... We have a superabundance of raw materials, a more than ample supply of equipment for manufacturing these materials into goods ... and transportation and commercial facilities for making them available to all who need them. But raw materials stand unused, factories stand idle, railroad traffic continues to dwindle, merchants sell less and less, while millions of able-bodied men and women ... are clamoring for the opportunity to work. This is the awful paradox with which we are confronted.

The country needs and ... demands bold, persistent experimentation. It is common sense to take a method and try it. If it fails, admit it frankly and try another. But above all, try something. The millions who are in want will not stand by silently forever.

—From "Address at Oglethorpe University," May 22, 1932.

KEY TERMS AND CONCEPTS

From FDR's Oglethorpe University address:

amenities Desirable features.

calamitous Catastrophic or disastrous.

clamor To loudly or forcefully demand.

mirage An illusion, or something that seems possible but is not.

paradox A contradiction.

prudent Careful or thoughtful about the future.

thrifty Cautious with money.

tragic irony A situation where one thing is expected but the opposite thing happens.

From FDR's first inaugural address:

curtailment Restriction or reduction.

endure To withstand suffering or to remain in existence.

foe Enemy.

prosper To be successful financially.

revive To come back to life or to an original state of being.

stricken Negatively affected or distressed.

CONSIDER THIS

1. What did graduates have to look forward to in 1928? In 1932?
2. What point was Roosevelt making about "easy money" versus thrift and prudence?
3. What does he mean by the "tragic irony" of the economy, and what is his prescription for a cure?

FDR's 1933 Inaugural Address

Months after delivering his address at Oglethorpe University, Roosevelt won the presidential election by a landslide. He was sworn in as president of the United States on March 4, 1933.

This March 1933 photo captures Hoover (*left*) and Roosevelt (*right*) riding to the US Capitol for Roosevelt's inauguration.

In this, his first inaugural address, FDR shows not only compassion for the American people and a promise of energetic national leadership, but also a great spirit. His words "the only thing we have to fear is fear itself" gave hope to millions and are among the most famous in US history.

> This is … the time to speak the truth, the whole truth, frankly and boldly. Nor need we shrink from honestly facing conditions in our country today. This great Nation will endure as it has endured, will revive and will prosper. So, first of all, let me assert my firm belief that the only thing we have to fear is fear itself …
>
> In such a spirit on my part and on yours we face our common difficulties … Values have shrunken to fantastic levels; taxes have risen; our ability to pay has fallen; government of all kinds is faced by serious curtailment of income; … farmers find no markets for their produce; the savings of many years in thousands of families are gone.
>
> More important, a host of unemployed citizens face the grim problem of existence, and an equally great number toil with little return …
>
> This Nation asks for action, and action now.
>
> Our greatest primary task is to put people to work … It can be accomplished in part by direct recruiting by the Government itself, treating the task as we would treat the emergency of war, but at the same time, through this employment, accomplishing greatly

FDR recognized that the Depression affected everyone—from the old to the young, from those who lived in cities to those who lived on farms, like these children.

needed projects to stimulate and reorganize the use of our natural resources ...

I am prepared under my constitutional duty to recommend the measures that a stricken Nation in the midst of a stricken world may require. These measures ... I shall seek, within my constitutional authority, to bring to speedy adoption.

In the event that the national emergency is still critical, I shall not evade the clear course of duty

> that will then confront me. I shall ask the Congress for … broad Executive power to wage a war against the emergency, as great as the power that would be given to me if we were in fact invaded by a foreign foe.
>
> —From Franklin Delano Roosevelt's first inaugural address, March 4, 1933.

CONSIDER THIS

1. What would be the first task of FDR's administration?
2. How do you think Roosevelt felt about Hoover's idea of rugged individualism?

Fireside Chats in Every Living Room

In the 1930s, almost every household in the United States had a radio. President Roosevelt understood the power of this vehicle for communication and used it regularly to share his policies with the American people. He called his radio talks "fireside chats."

In the following excerpt from his first talk, delivered from the White House on March 12, 1933, the president explains why he has called for a bank holiday. He had no choice. In February, the governor of Michigan had ordered the banks in his state closed for eight days. He called the closing a "bank holiday," but there was nothing festive about the event.

Such closings were desperate measures to keep people from withdrawing all of their money from the banks, which would cause the banks to collapse. When the Michigan banks closed, panic spread to other states. Soon people were rushing to their local banks and taking out their money, stuffing it in mattresses, under carpets, and in tin cans. In light of such events, FDR called for a national bank holiday.

FDR's fireside chats were broadcast across several radio networks. These broadcasts, which used informal language to discuss US government and policy, often provided Americans with hope.

Banks began to reopen on March 13 in a new atmosphere. They were placed under government supervision, and the amount of gold and currency flowing out of them was strictly regulated, or controlled. Depositors began to look at the banks as safe places for their money. The following is an excerpt from FDR's chat on the bank crisis.

> I want to talk for a few minutes with the people of the United States about banking … I want to tell you what has been done in the last few days, why it was done, and what the next steps are going to be.
>
> First of all let me state the simple fact that when you deposit money in a bank the bank does not put the money into a safe-deposit vault. It invests your money in many different forms of credit-bonds, commercial paper, mortgages and many other kinds of loans. In other words, the bank puts your money to work to keep the wheels of industry and of agriculture turning around. A comparatively small part of the money you put into the bank is kept in currency …
>
> What, then, happened during the last few days of February and the first few days of March? Because of undermined confidence on the part of the public, there was a general rush by a large portion of our population to turn bank deposits into currency or gold … a rush so great that the soundest banks could not get enough currency to meet the demand … It was … impossible to sell perfectly sound assets of a bank and convert them into cash except at panic prices far below their real value.

KEY TERMS AND CONCEPTS

From FDR's first fireside chat:
comparatively Relatively.
proclamation Official announcement or order.
undermined Weakened.

From FDR's congressional address:
enacted Made law or put into practice.
forestry The practice of maintaining and caring for forests.
soil erosion The movement of the upper layer of soil by wind or water, which can lead to less fertile soil and therefore fewer crops.

By the afternoon of March 3, scarcely a bank in the country was open to do business. Proclamations temporarily closing them in whole or in part had been issued by the governors in almost all the states.

It was then that I issued the proclamation providing for the nation-wide bank holiday, and this was the first step in the Government's reconstruction of our financial and economic fabric.

—From Franklin Delano Roosevelt, "On the Bank Crisis," March 12, 1933.

CONSIDER THIS

1. Why did people rush to withdraw their money from banks? What was the result of these "panic" withdrawals?
2. Why could the banks not immediately convert their assets into cash?

FDR's Unemployment Relief Plan

One of the first actions taken by the Roosevelt administration was providing relief for the unemployed. There were about fifteen million people without work in 1933. States and cities were unable to provide help to so many, and private charities had run out of funds. In this speech, delivered on March 21, 1933, FDR gives an overview of his plan to help the nation recover.

> To the Congress:
>
> It is essential to our recovery program that measures immediately be enacted aimed at unemployment relief. A direct attack in this problem suggests three types of legislation.
>
> The first is the enrollment of workers now by the Federal Government for such public employment as can be quickly started.
>
> The second is grants to States for relief work.
>
> The third extends to a broad public works labor-creating program.

> I propose to create a civilian conservation corps to be used in simple work not interfering with normal employment, and confining itself to forestry, the prevention of soil erosion, flood control, and similar projects.
>
> Control and direction of such work can be carried on by existing machinery of the departments of Labor, Agriculture, War and Interior.
>
> I estimate that 250,000 men can be given temporary employment by early summer if you give me authority to proceed within the next two weeks.
>
> —From *The Public Papers and Addresses of Franklin D. Roosevelt,* Vol. 2, 1933 (New York: Random House, 1938).

CONSIDER THIS

1. In his inaugural address, FDR had promised to "put people to work." In an earlier speech, to the graduating class at Oglethorpe University, he had advocated "bold, persistent experimentation." Do you think he was true to his word?

The Beginning of Change

With this congressional address, Franklin Delano Roosevelt's New Deal programs were underway. These programs would be responsible for bolstering, or strengthening, the US economy. The effects of these programs can still be seen in the United States. Some of the programs still even exist today.

This political cartoon depicts how many people were concerned about the amount of money that FDR was pumping into New Deal programs.

4 The New Deal

The New Deal refers to a series of federal programs implemented between 1933 and 1939 by Franklin Delano Roosevelt and Congress to provided economic relief during the Depression. The programs created jobs, protected workers' rights, aided businesses, and created and preserved public spaces. The changes made through these programs had lasting effects. However, Americans had a diverse set of responses to them.

The First New Deal

There were two different waves of legislation referred to as the New Deal. The first came in 1933, right after Roosevelt was inaugurated as president. With employment rates at an all-time low, Roosevelt's First New Deal focused on employing people through programs like the Civilian Conservation Corps and the Public Works Administration.

He also wanted to protect workers' rights through the National Recovery Administration.

The Second New Deal

Although these programs were successful in some ways, poverty and unemployment persisted, or continued. In spring 1935, Roosevelt passed a new round of legislation that created the Works Progress Administration, which was responsible for building many of the public buildings and roadways we still have today. Similarly, the Social Security Administration, which provides federal funds to people in need, was created during this second New Deal push.

Employment Programs

The United States Employment Service was organized in 1933 at the same time that government relief agencies were started. Many people thought the new organization would be only a temporary measure during a time of economic distress. However, the agency became a permanent fixture. Its job is to help match workers with employers through a collection of government-supported offices around the country. The following article appeared in the *Fort Wayne Journal-Gazette* in 1937, advising people how to use the new service.

> How does John or Jane Doe go about getting a job in Fort Wayne? One of his best bets will be to get in touch with the Indiana State Employment service if he or she is not already registered and included in the files of that far-reaching organization, an affiliate of the United States Employment Service ... It serves as a clearing house for labor, and when an employer makes a request for a specific type of man for a certain job, the employment office is concerned only

with the man in its files who has the ability and can meet the requirements of that job.

Here's a tip for applicants. It was found in digging for this story that the interviewers have an aversion for male applicants who are unshaven, and girls who snap their gum [or] wear brilliant nail polish ...

—From Robert D. Adams, "John Doe Gets His Job Through the Indiana State Employment Service," in the *Fort Wayne Journal-Gazette*, October 3, 1937.

CONSIDER THIS

1. According to the article, what specific benefits did the service provide to job applicants? To employers?
2. Have "tips" for job applicants changed much since the time this was written?

The Civilian Conservation Corps Raises Spirits

The Civilian Conservation Corps (CCC) was established in March 1933. It was one of the first and most successful of the New Deal programs. It gave work to hundreds of thousands of young men aged eighteen to twenty-five. CCC workers were organized like an army and were put to work in a variety of ways. They planted trees in national parks, created trails, and built roads. They also planted grasses on damaged hillsides and dug irrigation ditches through which water could be transported and moved in arid, or dry, regions.

The CCC employed about three million men during its nine years of existence. For many of these men, it provided an opportunity to continue their education and learn self-discipline.

In the United States, people still benefit from the work the CCC undertook to develop and maintain national parks and forests. Here, two CCC workers build a fence in Pisgah National Forest in North Carolina.

In the following selection, Robert L. Miller recalls what being part of the CCC meant to him. He was in his early twenties when he joined.

> There is no need to mention much of my life before I enrolled in the Civilian Conservation Corps ... I was often hungry, and almost constantly broke.
>
> When I finally enrolled in this great enterprise at Sacramento, California, in October, 1933, I was conscious of just one thing—I would be fed, clothed and sheltered during the coming winter. Also I would receive enough actual cash each month to provide the few luxuries I desired.
>
> The two weeks I had to wait between the time I enrolled and the day we were to leave for camp were given over to much thinking ... Several questions flashed through my mind. Would I make friends with my fellow members? What kind of work would I be doing? Would I be able to "take it"? This last question was by far the most important to me.
>
> Let me pause for a moment to give you a short character analysis of myself. For years ... I could not overcome the feeling that I was just a little inferior to my fellow men. I did not credit myself with the quality of a leader among men ... It was in this frame of mind that I joined seventy other young men on the morning of October 26, to leave for our camp in the Sierra Nevada Mountains ...

Early in November we moved to our winter camp near Hayward, California. During the period of camp construction that followed our move, I was put in charge of several small jobs. They were insignificant in their nature, but it did me a lot of good just to think that I was considered reliable enough to boss even a small project ...

[Several months] later news came to camp that an Educational Advisor was coming to camp to direct the boys in their pursuit of education. Also we heard that some man in camp was to be appointed to the newly created position of Assistant Educational Advisor. This new position was to carry an assistant leader's rating, which meant a raise in pay ... On April 6, our Educational Advisor arrived in camp, and that evening I was told I had been appointed his assistant. My goal had been reached ...

I shall try to convey to you just what the Civilian Conservation Corps has meant to me ... First of all, by enrolling in President Roosevelt's peace-time army, I managed to retain my self respect. I did not have to become either a parasite, living off my relatives, or a professional bum. It gave me a chance to stand on my own two feet and make my own way in the world. Then it gave me the opportunity to make friendships that will live forever.

—From Robert L. Miller, "It's a Great Life," in National Archives and Records Administration, Record Group 35, Division of Selection, Success Stories, 1937.

KEY TERMS AND CONCEPTS

From Robert L. Miller's account:

retain To keep or maintain.

From the Tennessee Valley Authority Act:

acquire To obtain.

board of directors A group of people that oversees an organization or business.

body corporate A corporation or company.

condemn To officially declare that something privately owned must be given up for government use.

eminent domain The right to take away private property for government use.

transmission line A line through which electricity is sent.

tributary Small river or stream that flows into a larger river.

From Lorena Hickok's letter:

authoritative Reliable.

eke To make a small amount.

furnish To provide.

illiteracy The inability to read or write.

marginal land Land that produces only a few profitable crops.

prolonged undernourishment A long time without enough food.

rehabilitation The act of restoring something.

squalor Extremely dirty or unpleasant, especially because of poverty.

stunted Undersized.

submarginal land Land that does not produce profitable crops.

table land High, flat land.

trade A job that requires a specific set of skills or special training.

wretchedness Poor or unfortunate state.

CONSIDER THIS

1. What personal goals did Miller hope to achieve in the CCC?
2. Why do you think he was selected for a leadership role?
3. The CCC was abolished in 1942. Do you think such an organization might have value today? Why or why not?

The Tennessee Valley Authority

The Tennessee Valley Authority (TVA) was one of the largest and most controversial projects of the New Deal. The TVA came into being on May 18, 1933. Its purpose was to bring flood control and electricity to the people living in the Tennessee River basin. The region, which is approximately 41,000 square miles (106,200 square

Though the Wilson Dam on the Tennessee River had been completed in 1924, it became central to the TVA's work in the region during the Depression.

kilometers) in area, includes parts of Tennessee, Kentucky, Virginia, North Carolina, Georgia, Alabama, and Mississippi. A series of dams, which produced electricity, and reservoirs, artificial lakes often resulting from the creation of dams, were constructed on land taken over by the federal government. The long-range goals of the TVA were the improvement of agriculture and the industrialization of this economically depressed region.

Opponents of the TVA believed that it was not the role of the federal government to be involved in developing and distributing electrical power. They held that such an enterprise put the government in competition with private utility companies, whose role it should be.

Some people also argued that projects like the TVA would bring the United States a step closer to a state-planned economy like that found under communism in the Soviet Union. The government of the Soviet Union owned the means of production, deciding what products to produce, how and when to produce them, and how much to charge for them. Free and open competition did not exist under the Soviet system. Communism frightened many Americans who worried that capitalism, where private businesses as opposed to the government control the country's industry, would be threatened by power companies owned and operated by the government.

Despite these people's concerns, the Tennessee Valley Authority opened its doors. In fact, it still exists today. The following is an excerpt from the Tennessee Valley Authority Act, which created the TVA.

> Be it enacted by the Senate and House of Representatives of the United States of America in Congress assembled, that for the purpose of maintaining and operating the properties now owned by the United States in the vicinity of Muscle Shoals, Alabama, in the interest of the national defense and for agriculture and industrial development, and to

improve navigation in the Tennessee River and to control the destructive flood waters in the Tennessee River and Mississippi River Basins, there is hereby created a body corporate by the name of "Tennessee Valley Authority" (hereinafter referred to as the "Corporation") ...

The board of directors of the Corporation ... shall be composed of three members, to be appointed by the President, by and with the advice and consent of the Senate. In appointing the members of the board, the President shall designate the chairman. All other officials, agents, and employees shall be designated and selected by the board ...

The board ... shall have power to acquire real estate for the construction of dams, reservoirs, transmission lines, power houses, and other structures, and navigation projects at any point along the Tennessee River, or any of its tributaries, and in the event that the owner or owners of such property shall fail and refuse to sell to the Corporation at a price deemed fair and reasonable by the board, then the Corporation may proceed to exercise the right of eminent domain, and to condemn all property that it deems necessary for carrying out the purposes of this Act.

The President shall, from time to time ... recommend to Congress such legislation as he deems proper to carry out ... for the economic and social well-being of the people living in said river basin.

—From Tennessee Valley Authority Act, May 18, 1933.

CONSIDER THIS

1. The law of eminent domain—the right of the government to take over private property for public use—is based on the belief that the government, representing the welfare of the people as a whole, has greater power than the individual. According to the law, the government must pay the individual owner a fair price for the property taken. If the owner refuses to sell, the government may "condemn" the land and have a fair price determined by an appraiser, or someone who sets the price or value of something, which the owner must accept. Do you think that the law of eminent domain is fair?
2. Do you support the idea of the Tennessee Valley Authority? Why or why not?

Report from the Tennessee River Valley

Lorena Hickok was a journalist who worked for Harry Hopkins, the head of the Federal Emergency Relief Administration (FERA) and a close adviser to President Roosevelt. FERA coordinated the federal government's assistance to the states to help the jobless. Hopkins asked Hickok to be his confidential investigator and to gather information about the everyday lives of those affected by the Depression. Hopkins wanted to know everything, the bad as well as the good.

For more than two years, Hickok traveled across thirty states and reported to Hopkins on what she saw. The following letter recounts Hickok's impression of the Tennessee River Valley and the changes brought about by the TVA.

In addition to working for FERA, Lorena Hickok (*left*) was a close friend to Eleanor Roosevelt (*right*). They are shown here on a trip to the US Virgin Islands, with Paul Pearson (*center*), the islands' governor.

Florence, Alabama
June 6, 1934

Dear Mr. Hopkins:

A Promised Land, bathed in golden sunlight, is rising out of the grey shadows of want and squalor and wretchedness down here in the Tennessee Valley these days.

Ten thousand men are at work, building with timber and steel and concrete the New Deal's most magnificent project.

Thousands of them are residents of the Valley, working five and a half hours a day, five days a week, for a really LIVING wage. Houses are going up for them to live in—better houses than they have ever had in their lives before. And in their leisure time they are studying—farming, trades, the art of living, preparing themselves for the fuller lives they are to lead in that Promised Land ...

With TVA getting up standards in rehabilitation, the rest of the state has got a long, long way to go.

Out of nearly 70,000 families on relief in Tennessee, probably 30,000 or more live in small towns or in the country. Many of these are in abandoned lumber and mining camps. Most of them who are farmers apparently are living on submarginal or marginal land.

Fairly typical ... was a district I visited yesterday. Table land. Thin soil. Terrible housing. Illiteracy.

Evidence of prolonged undernourishment. No knowledge of how to live decently or farm profitably if they had decent land.

"Five years is about as long as you can get any crop on this land," one farmer told me. "Then it's gone and you have to clear some more and start over again."

Crops grown on it are stunted. Corn ... grows only about a third as tall there as it does in Iowa. They tell me it isn't even good timber land. Just a thin coating of soil over rock. A county agent said it might make good orchard land, but any farming operation there should be under skilled supervision with authority to make farmers do as they were told.

Eastern Tennessee is worse ... There you see ... evidence of what happens when you cut timber off mountain sides and plant crops there. There are great "bald patches" of rock on those mountains!

What to do with these people makes a nice little problem. Whether to move them off—and, if so, where to put them—or, on table land, for instance, where with careful and authoritative supervision they might eke out a living, leave them there and take a chance on their being absorbed in the industries that should be attracted down here by the cheap power furnished by TVA.

—From Richard Lowitt and Maurine Beasley, eds., *One Third of a Nation: Lorena Hickok Reports on the Great Depression* (Urbana, IL: University of Illinois Press, 1981).

CONSIDER THIS

1. Throughout the Great Depression, people disagreed about the role of government. Should government play a powerful part in controlling business, agriculture, and people's personal lives? Or should it stay far away and let everyone freely go about their lives and jobs, no matter the social costs? How does Hickok's report reflect the attitude of the Roosevelt administration on this issue?
2. What particular words does she use that give us clues to her own feelings about the New Deal?

The Short-Lived National Recovery Administration

On June 16, 1933, President Roosevelt signed the National Industrial Recovery Act. This act established the National Recovery Administration (NRA), a government agency intended to help business and industry. The NRA would enforce codes of fair business practices, which would be drawn up by representatives of companies within major industries.

Although the codes were meant primarily to aid business and industry, they also addressed concerns of the working man. The codes set minimum wages, or pay rates, and the maximum hours a person could work. They also supported the right of workers to organize themselves into labor unions. Prior to the formation of the NRA, the government had little say over business practices. Companies could compete freely, for better or worse. With the NRA, the government assumed greater control over private industry.

During its brief life, the NRA was involved in the drawing up of more than five hundred codes of fair practice. Its symbol was the Blue Eagle, which businesses were urged to display in their offices and factories as a sign of their participation. Consumers were urged to do business only with those stores and shops that displayed the Blue Eagle.

Opponents of the NRA called it authoritarian, or too strict. In 1935, the Supreme Court declared it unconstitutional. President Roosevelt ended the NRA shortly thereafter. Several sections of the National Industrial Recovery Act follow.

> Sec. 1 A national emergency productive of widespread unemployment and disorganization of industry, which burdens interstate and foreign commerce, affects the public welfare, and undermines the standards of living of the American people, is hereby declared to exist ...
>
> Sec. 3 Upon application to the President by one or more trade or industrial associations or groups, the President may approve a code or codes of fair competition for the trade or industry.
>
> Sec. 7 ... Employees shall have the right to organize and bargain collectively through representatives of their own choosing, and shall be free from the interference, restraint, or coercion of employers.
>
> —From Henry Steele Commager, ed., "U.S. Statutes at Large," in *Documents of American History*, Vol. XLVIII (New York: Appleton-Century-Crofts, 1963).

KEY TERMS AND CONCEPTS

From the National Industrial Recovery Act:

bargain collectively To negotiate, or seek an agreement, as a group of workers rather than individually; also referred to as "collective bargaining."

coercion The act of persuading someone through the use of threats.

interstate Between more than one state.

From Beniamino Benvenuto Bufano's essay:

renaissance A renewed interest in something.

From Eleanor Roosevelt's column:

municipal Relating to a city.

CONSIDER THIS

1. The National Industrial Recovery Act starts out by declaring that the nation was in a state of emergency. What significance does this statement have for the following sections of the law?
2. Why would employers be opposed to labor unions? Are unions still important today?
3. Why do you think the NRA was found unconstitutional?

Artists Celebrate the Works Progress Administration

The Works Progress Administration (WPA) was established in 1935 as part of FDR's New Deal. It was renamed the Work Projects Administration in 1939. The WPA was headed by Harry Hopkins, and its goal was to provide jobs for the unemployed on public works projects. The WPA was responsible for thousands of building projects, including roads, libraries, and airports. More than eight million people were put to work by the WPA.

The Federal Art Project (FAP) was part of the WPA, as were the Federal Writers' Project and the Federal Theatre Project. Artists working under the FAP created murals for the nation's libraries, post offices, and courthouses. They also sculpted statues and decorative figures for city parks. In return, the government paid them a salary of between twenty-three dollars and forty-two dollars per week. The artists supplied their own materials whenever possible. By working for the FAP, artists survived and created beautiful art for the public. In the following excerpt, San Francisco–based sculptor Beniamino Benvenuto Bufano explains what the WPA meant to him.

Lucile Lloyd, working for the Federal Art Project, completes a mural titled *The Origin and Development of the Name of the State of California.*

Long before the WPA/FAP came into existence, I offered my services to several communities at day-labor wages if they would supply the materials and let me work. There must have been many artists with this same spirit. Movements like a government art project are not an accident; they come from great needs, the need of the artist to give something to the world as much as from his need to survive. We need artists who are interested in creating a universal culture. In being alive. In having something to say. And in saying it—ready to consider no sacrifice too great in making themselves heard. Artists who are concerned with universal truths. WPA/FAP has laid the foundation of a renaissance of art in America. It is the open sesame to a freer art and a more democratic use of the creations of the artist's hand and brain. It has freed American art ... For the present we have steel, stone, and tools. We have the spirit of great men and great cities to move us. We are busy.

—From Beniamino Benvenuto Bufano, an essay written in 1936 for a proposed report to Congress on the value of the WPA/FAP in the file "Federal Support for the Visual Arts: The New Deal and Now," Library of the National Collection of Fine Arts of the Smithsonian Institution, Washington, DC.

CONSIDER THIS

1. According to the writer, why does an artist need to work?
2. What might this artist have meant by saying the FAP had made possible a freer, more democratic art?
3. Should the government support the creation of art, both in times of wealth and during a depression? Why or why not?

Eleanor Roosevelt's Day and the Milwaukee Handicraft Project

Eleanor Roosevelt was the eyes and ears of the president. She went places her husband could not and told him about what she learned. In the following excerpt from My Day, her regular newspaper column, the First Lady recalls a trip to the Milwaukee WPA Handicraft Project. Here, unemployed women made dolls, books, rugs, quilts, and other household items. The handicrafts were sold to schools, hospitals, and theaters for the cost of the materials. The project started in 1935 and employed five thousand women and minorities before ending in 1943. The women who took part earned about fifty dollars a month.

> My Day: November 12, 1936, by Eleanor Roosevelt
>
> I have just come back from one of the most interesting mornings I have ever spent. Milwaukee has a handicraft project for unskilled women ... They are doing artistic work under most able teachers ... These women have had few educational advantages and were so unskilled that they were rejected on the sewing project ... One woman made her own design for a piece of work which I much admired and she had had just three years in school.
>
> They are binding scrap books for children; books to be used in hospitals; and books for the Braille project ... They [also] make rugs and hangings all of original design.

> They are making dolls as attractive as any I have seen ... They are making costumes for public schools and institutions and the Municipal opera ... The schools provide the materials [and] two young people with art training who have not yet found jobs do the research and designs. The costumes remain as a permanent theatrical wardrobe in the schools or institutions to which they are sent.
>
> We visited a very fine sewing room for women where about nine hundred are employed. The working conditions are excellent and they have an opportunity to work on all types of modern machines, which is a help to future employment. Only five percent of the workers had any training before they entered this work room.
>
> —From Eleanor Roosevelt, My Day, November 12, 1936.

CONSIDER THIS

1. In what ways did the Milwaukee Handicraft Project help the women who participated?

A Rabbi Writes to the President

In 1935, FDR wrote a letter to the nation's religious leaders in which he asked them to report about conditions in their communities. The White House received hundreds of replies. Here, a rabbi voices his thoughts to the president about the WPA and how it was working in his city.

Dear Mr. Roosevelt:

For about two years now I have been the supervisor of a project first in Work Relief and then under the Works Progress Administration ...

This has brought me into direct contact with the very people for whom the ... Works Program has been intended. I wish that those who are opposing such a program could meet these people[:] ... old people who have worked hard all their lives, only to face desperate need in their old age; ... middle-aged workers cast adrift not through their own incapability, but [through that] of those who employed them; ... young people who have just completed their education and find that the working world has no place for them. I have found some shirkers and cheaters, but they are a very small minority; and the thing that has impressed me is the eagerness with which the unemployed seek for work, even the most difficult.

As for the Works Program itself, I find that while it has been nobly conceived, it is often ineptly administered ... There is still great difficulty in fitting the right man to the job. I have sat for days at the central clearing offices, and know what I am talking about. Time after time I have been sent people who are absolutely disqualified for my work, just because no one else knows what to do with them; while on the other hand, those for whom I asked and whom I knew would be both serviceable to me and happy in the work are the very ones that I have been unable to obtain.

In conclusion, a personal word. Do not be afraid of what is written by those who are afraid of change, … or by those who are offended because you do not act upon their own pet peeve. The masses of the people are still with you and you are their hope.

Yours sincerely,

Rabbi Simon Cohen
Brooklyn, NY

—From "Letters from the Nation's Clergy," October 27, 1935, FDR Library, President's Personal File, Entry 21, Box 22.

CONSIDER THIS

1. In his work for the WPA, what has impressed the rabbi most?
2. What is his main criticism of the program?

Huey Long Goes a Step Further

Franklin Roosevelt wasn't the only political leader with a plan to get the nation back on its feet during the Great Depression. Huey Long was a powerful Democratic senator from Louisiana. At first Long was a supporter of FDR, but he came to think that Roosevelt was not going far enough to change the nation's economic policies.

KEY TERMS AND CONCEPTS

From Rabbi Simon Cohen's letter:
ineptly Without skill.
shirkers People who avoid responsibility.

From Huey Long's speech:
big concerns Large businesses or financial investments.
render To make.
surplus An excess; extra.
toil Hard physical labor.

Long had his own program to help the country. It was called Share Our Wealth. Long called for the elimination of all personal wealth over $5 million and a government-guaranteed annual minimum income of $5,000 for each family. In addition, Long proposed old-age pensions, or regular payments to someone who is retired. He also proposed a program of public works, in which people worked on buildings, schools, and roads. Additionally, he proposed a minimum wage for workers and a shorter work week.

Huey Long gave a speech in the Senate on February 5, 1934, in which he described the Share Our Wealth program. Part of his speech is included here.

> People of America: In every community get together at once and organize a share-our-wealth society—Motto: Every man a king.

Principles and platform:

1. To limit poverty by providing that every deserving family shall share in the wealth of America for not less than one third of the average wealth, thereby to possess not less than $5,000 free of debt.

2. To limit fortunes to such a few million dollars as will allow the balance of the American people to share in the wealth and profits of the land.

3. Old-age pensions of $30 per month to persons over 60 years of age who do not earn as much as $1,000 per year or who possess less than $10,000 in cash or property, thereby to remove from the field of labor in times of unemployment those who have contributed their share to the public service.

4. To limit the hours of work to such an extent as to prevent overproduction and to give the workers of America some share in the recreations, conveniences, and luxuries of life.

5. To balance agricultural production with what can be sold and consumed according to the laws of God, which have never failed.

6. To care for the veterans of our wars.

7. Taxation to run the Government to be supported, first, by reducing big fortunes from the top, thereby to improve the country and provide employment in public works whenever agricultural surplus is such

as to render unnecessary, in whole or in part, any particular crop.

Simple and Concrete—Not an Experiment

To share our wealth by providing for every deserving family to have one third of the average wealth would mean that ... such a family could have a fairly comfortable home, an automobile, and a radio, with other reasonable home conveniences, and a place to educate their children. Through sharing the work, that is, by limiting the hours of toil so that all would share in what is made and produced in the land, every family would have enough coming in every year to feed, clothe, and provide a fair share of the luxuries of life to its members.

There would be no limit to opportunity. One might become a millionaire or more. There would be a chance for talent to make a man big, because enough would be floating in the land to give brains its chance to be used. As it is, no matter how smart a man may be, everything is tied up in so few hands that no amount of energy or talent has a chance to gain any of it.

Would it break up big concerns? No. It would simply mean that, instead of one man getting all the one concern made, that there might be 1,000 or 10,000 persons sharing in such excess fortune, any one of whom, or all of whom, might be millionaires and over.

I ask somebody in every city, town, village, and farm community of America to take this as my personal request to call a meeting of as many neighbors and friends as will come to it to start a share-our-wealth society. Elect a president and a secretary and charge no dues. The meeting can be held at a courthouse, in some town hall or public building, or in the home of someone.

It does not matter how many will come to the first meeting. Get a society organized, if it has only two members. Then let us get to work quick, quick, quick to put an end by law to people starving and going naked in this land of too much to eat and too much to wear.

We have waited long enough for … financial masters to do these things. They have promised and promised. Now we find our country $10 billion further in debt on account of the depression, and big lenders even propose to get 90 percent of that out of the hides of the common people in the form of a sales tax.

There is nothing wrong with the United States. We have more food than we can eat. We have more clothes and things out of which to make clothes than we can wear. We have more houses and lands than the whole 120 million can use if they all had good homes. So what is the trouble? Nothing except that a handful of men have everything and the balance of the people have nothing if their debts were paid. There should be every man a king in this land flowing with milk and honey instead of the lords of finance at the top and slaves and peasants at the bottom.

—From Senator Huey Long, speech before the Senate, February 5, 1934, advocating his Share Our Wealth program, Congressional Record, February 5, 1934.

CONSIDER THIS

1. In Long's opinion, who is responsible for the nation's problems? Why?
2. Long suggests that limits be placed on individual wealth. Does his idea correspond to traditional American ideals?

Not a Good Deal for Everyone

Even though the New Deal brought programs and relief early in the decade of the Great Depression, people continued to struggle to find work and feed their families. In 1937, the country slipped into a recession, or a short-lived downturn in the economy.

The prices of goods dropped during the Great Depression as many people could barely afford the essentials.

5 Poverty Persists

During the Great Depression, Americans got by on very little money or did without the necessities of life. Wages fell from almost twenty-five dollars per week in 1929 for manufacturing jobs to sixteen dollars per week for the same job in 1933. It was difficult to survive on these wages when, in 1933, bread sold for seven cents a loaf, eggs for twenty-nine cents a dozen, and milk for ten cents a quart.

Struggling to Survive

People who were out of work tried to find odd jobs such as mowing lawns or painting fences to get enough money to buy food. Many families planted vegetable gardens and ate what they were able to grow. In some very poor families, children took turns eating. People tried to help each other by giving away their leftover food to the needy.

Here, a sharecropper's son picks cotton to help make ends meet. Sharecroppers are people who pay a portion of the rent for the land on which they live and farm with the crops they produce.

It was simply not enough, and even New Deal relief programs did not completely erase poverty from the United States. Accepting relief (as welfare, or financial support from the government, was called in the 1930s) was degrading to many. The unemployed preferred to work instead of taking a government handout.

Children of the Depression

Many of the poor people during the Depression were children. They had few or no toys and sometimes no food or clothing. Those who stayed in school often went there hungry and weak. Some boys and girls chose to stay home because they were embarrassed by their worn clothing.

Many children had to work to help support their families. These children dropped out of school to work in mills, mines, and other places that hired seasonal, part-time, or temporary workers.

These child workers received small wages for their work, which they turned over to their parents. Ashamed of not being able to help out their parents, older children left home and school behind and wandered the countryside by foot or by rail.

Child labor was common in the 1930s, even after the passage of the Fair Labor Standards Act of 1938. This act set a minimum age of eighteen for dangerous occupations, sixteen for company jobs done during school hours, and fourteen for nonmanufacturing jobs done after school hours. The money brought in by a young worker was often the difference between his or her family's eating or not. Many older children lied about their ages to get work.

For employers, young workers were easy to hire and fire because no one expected them to speak out about poor treatment. They were also paid less than adult workers.

A Farmer's Struggles

Farmers were also among the hardest hit by the Depression. Never rich, they lived from season to season, usually in debt to banks and loan holders for their livestock or farm machinery. When crops failed or natural disasters such as drought or tornadoes wiped out their efforts, they had no place to turn. Many of the farmers in the poorest regions of the United States became migrant laborers, or people who move from place to place for work, during the 1930s. Whole families traveled from region to region, harvesting crops for next to nothing.

Farmers had been suffering from economic hardship long before the stock market crash of 1929. Low prices for crops, years of drought, and continual debt had placed the nation's small farmers in conditions of poverty or near-poverty before the hard times of the 1930s arrived. In the following letter to President Roosevelt, a Texas farmer explains his situation.

> I own my own little home and a few live stock ... I have them all mortgaged to a man and he is fixing to foreclose me.
>
> I have done all I could to pay the note ... I fell short on my crop this time and he didn't allow me even one nickel ... to feed myself ... I have a wife and three little children ...
>
> I am asking you for help of some kind please.
>
> From Robert S. McElvaine, ed., *Down and Out in the Great Depression: Letters from the Forgotten Man* (Chapel Hill, NC: University of North Carolina Press, 1983).

CONSIDER THIS

1. Do you think Roosevelt could help this man? If so, how?

A Frustrated WPA Worker

Even though the New Deal programs were helpful, not everyone was happy with them. For instance, not every person taking part in the WPA was happy with the program, especially when relief checks did not come on time.

Accepting relief in the form of welfare payments bothered many Americans. They were brought up to believe in the importance of self-reliance and hard work and wanted nothing more than a job. To many on relief, the payments were also too small to make much of a difference in their lives. They were still living in poverty.

KEY TERMS AND CONCEPTS

From a Texas farmer's letter:

fixing Planning.

foreclose To take back property that has been mortgaged, or loaned.

From Eluard Luchell McDaniel's account:

box car A freight car of a train.

Bull An informal word for a guard.

floater An informal word a vagrant, or someone without a home.

I-O-U An abbreviation for "I owe you."

petered out Ran out.

Here, a man from Union City, New Jersey, shares his frustrations with Harry Hopkins, who administered several of the New Deal's programs.

> … I am sick and tired of starving after I have done my share … to feed and take care of my family. What I … earn is barely enough … until the next check.
>
> From Robert S. McElvaine, ed., *Down and Out in the Great Depression: Letters from the Forgotten Man* (Chapel Hill, NC: University of North Carolina Press, 1983).

Here, Eleanor Roosevelt discusses WPA plans to convert a dump into a park. Despite the goals of federal projects like this one, people remained frustrated with "big government" and the poverty that persisted.

CONSIDER THIS

1. How do you think Hopkins felt about receiving a letter like this? What do you think he did in response?

One Hobo's Story

The Depression uprooted many Americans. They drifted from state to state looking for work. Some, having given up on the idea of finding work, drifted because there was nothing else to do. In 1933, there were between one and two million people on the road.

Adult men made up the majority of these "hoboes," migrant workers or homeless people without jobs. There were young hoboes too. More than two hundred thousand young Americans were homeless in the early years of the Depression. Many were school dropouts who lived by their wits on the streets, surviving on handouts and even stealing.

Others took to traveling around the countryside, taking rides from strangers or riding freight trains. Riding freight trains was especially dangerous. It was illegal, and if caught by the rail-yard guards, the offender could be beaten, jailed, or both.

Towns and cities did not welcome hoboes. The police warned them to "keep moving." The following description of "riding the rails" was written by Eluard Luchell McDaniel. He was fourteen years old when the events described here took place.

> In the winter of 1931, three bums and myself began to see California by a I-O-U. About twenty-five cents among the four of us. Sleeping in the most comfortable box cars in the Southern Pacific Railroad yard. There were no hotels in the city of Los Angeles for the price we had to pay ...
>
> At that time the hitch-hiking was not so good. People were afraid to trust strangers in their automobiles. The people that would give anyone a ride, did not want their car dirtyed up by bums like us. We done most of our traveling by train. In the railroad yard floaters were from all parts of America. The railroad Bulls were plentiful. They stayed busy trying to keep bums from riding the trains. Policemen were busy ordering floaters out of towns throughout California.
>
> Some of the guys was from California, [but] most came from the North, South, and East. There was no trouble to find gangs from everywhere. Some floaters could tell you every railroad stop from the Atlantic to the Pacific. There were four in our group:

> Luchell McDaniel, B. Jay Hubert, Asti Butt Slim, and Mulligan Joe ...
>
> The railroad Bull put us off the trains from Los Angeles ... We seen a milepost. It showed six miles from Los Angeles city limit, on the road ... and no stops. Not one had enough money to buy food for the group. We were saving the twenty-five cents for ferry fare into San Francisco. When we were three miles past San Bernardino, Asti spied some farmer's ranch. That ranch had peaches, grapes, and apricots. We made ourselves at home. We had our pockets full.
>
> We rode the Fireball Special for three hours and twenty minutes. Another unhappy stop. Most of the fruit from the ranch had almost petered out. Not much high talking and laughing. No one cared about how large New York was, or how small the next town. The talk were food.
>
> —From Eluard Luchell McDaniel, *Bumming in California* (New York: The Viking Press, 1937).

CONSIDER THIS

1. Why do you think the vagrants were treated the way they were?

A Teenager's Plea

Eleanor Roosevelt received numerous requests for help from the poor and unemployed. Many of the letters came from children and teenage boys and girls whose parents were barely able to give them food and clothes. Toys, bicycles, and sports equipment were simply beyond the means of many families, but boys and girls of course still longed for them. In the following letter, a teenage boy asks Mrs. Roosevelt for help.

> 42-06 159 Street
> Flushing, New York
> Mar. 22, 1934
>
> Dear Mrs. Roosevelt,
>
> Please excuse the paper. I have never asked anybody for anything before and I feel kind of awkward writing this.
>
> I am in the second term in Flushing High School and have managed to buy notebooks and pad so far. This being the spring term spring football is in session. This being my favorite sport I am trying out for the team. I managed to loan from a boy friend shoulder pad, helmit, and football pants but he didn't have any luck in securing a pair of football shoes. Practise started yesterday.
>
> I wore snickers and had my ankle cut by a fellow with shoe's on. I came home last night and spoke to my parents about getting a pair of shoes.
>
> I'm sure they would like me to have these but my father, who works three days a week makes only $13.44 on the Long Island State Park Commission said we could not afford them.
>
> I thought one of your sons may have an old pair of football shoes they do not use now. I wear size eight.

Please answer even if you can't do anything for me.

Thanking you in advance,

C. K.

—From *Dear Mrs. Roosevelt: The Letters.* Available at the New Deal Network: http://newdeal.feri.org/eleanor.

CONSIDER THIS

1. How do you think Mrs. Roosevelt responded to this letter? How would you have responded if you were her?

Boys in the Mines

Coal miners were among the poorest and most abused workers in America before and during the Depression. Working under the most dangerous conditions for insufficient wages, the miners were near slaves to the coal companies. They lived in company-built houses, were paid in company-issued money, and were forced to buy their food and supplies in company-owned stores, where prices were high. Their situation worsened during the 1930s when coal companies cut back production and shortened work hours.

In this excerpt, miner Fred Harrison describes his experiences as a child laborer in the drift coal mines of northern Missouri during the 1930s. A drift mine is an underground mine that has a horizontal or somewhat horizontal opening. Often these mines are built into hillsides at a downward slant. The roof, already low, gets lower as the mine goes farther into the hill. Miners crawl on their stomachs to get at the coal, which they place in a low car and push along in front of them.

This 1955 photo depicts men at the entrance of a drift mine, one of the main methods for developing an underground mine.

> I began in the drift mine when I was twelve. According to law, you must be sixteen before you start, but … a miner can take his son … Many a boy begins … when he's nine or ten … He can pick up chunks [of coal] and put them in a car being loaded, and he can fetch prop-caps when his old man is putting in a narrow cutting or using the riddle …
>
> The riddle is a coarse sieve through which the fine coal is sifted, the fine stuff falling to the ground to be shoveled separately into a car … The riddle man usually sits cross-legged, and for the greenhorn it's an extra-tiring job having to sit there and feel the shock of each shovelful of coal thrown into it. . . .
>
> The air [in the mine] is bad … and it makes you sleepy and gives you a headache …
>
> —From Ann Banks, *First-Person America* (New York: Alfred A. Knopf, 1980).

CONSIDER THIS

1. How do you think the work in the mines affected men's overall health? Do you think it had more or less of an effect on young boys?

Hired Hands

Joblessness forced many men and women to leave their homes and travel the nation in search of work. Country people moved to the cities in hope of getting jobs. Similarly, city people roamed around the countryside looking for the same. Oftentimes, the

KEY TERMS AND CONCEPTS

From Fred Harrison's account:

greenhorn A new worker.

prop-caps Supports used to hold up the roof of a mine.

sieve A mesh strainer.

From John Macnamara's account:

net profit The amount of money actually made after expenses like food.

Newburgh A city on the Hudson River about 50 miles (80 kilometers) north of New York City.

From Carl M. Mydans's report:

assembly line A series of workers working together to gradually assemble an item.

knack off To stop work.

payoffs weren't great. In the following selection, John Macnamara recalls his summer spent picking berries in New York State.

> After nine months of searching for a job in New York [City], I took to the road with two dollars in my pocket ... In the middle of July I reached Newburgh ... The local newspaper said that berry pickers were wanted at a place seven miles [11 kilometers] up the river. I arrived at dusk and the farmer said: "A cent and a half a quart. You feed yourself ..."

> I worked seven days and then took to the road again, with a net profit of ninety-eight cents.
>
> —From "Berry Picker," *Nation*, September 12, 1934.

CONSIDER THIS

1. Do you think the author thought his trip to Newburgh was worth the effort?

Life on the Assembly Line

The 1930s were marked by episodes of violent labor unrest, despite the National Industrial Recovery Act's protection of workers' right to organize and the setting of minimum wages and maximum hours. In the view of many workers, the act did not go far enough. A wave of strikes, or protests where employees refuse to work until their needs are met, followed its passage.

In 1934, there were 1,800 work stoppages involving more than 1.4 million workers. They included assembly-line workers, book and magazine editors, textile workers, and others. Playwright Clifford Odets even wrote a play about a strike called *Waiting for Lefty*.

American industrial workers, especially those in automobile assembly plants, were upset over wages, shutdowns, hiring practices, and working conditions. Above all, they demanded the right to bargain collectively with their employers. However, employers refused to talk with the labor unions and instead formed company unions. Employment was based on membership in the company union. Workers' unions went on strike to pressure businesses into meeting their demands. In the following selection from a 1933 investigative report by Carl M. Mydans, the writer describes why the workers at a Ford Motor Car assembly plant went on strike.

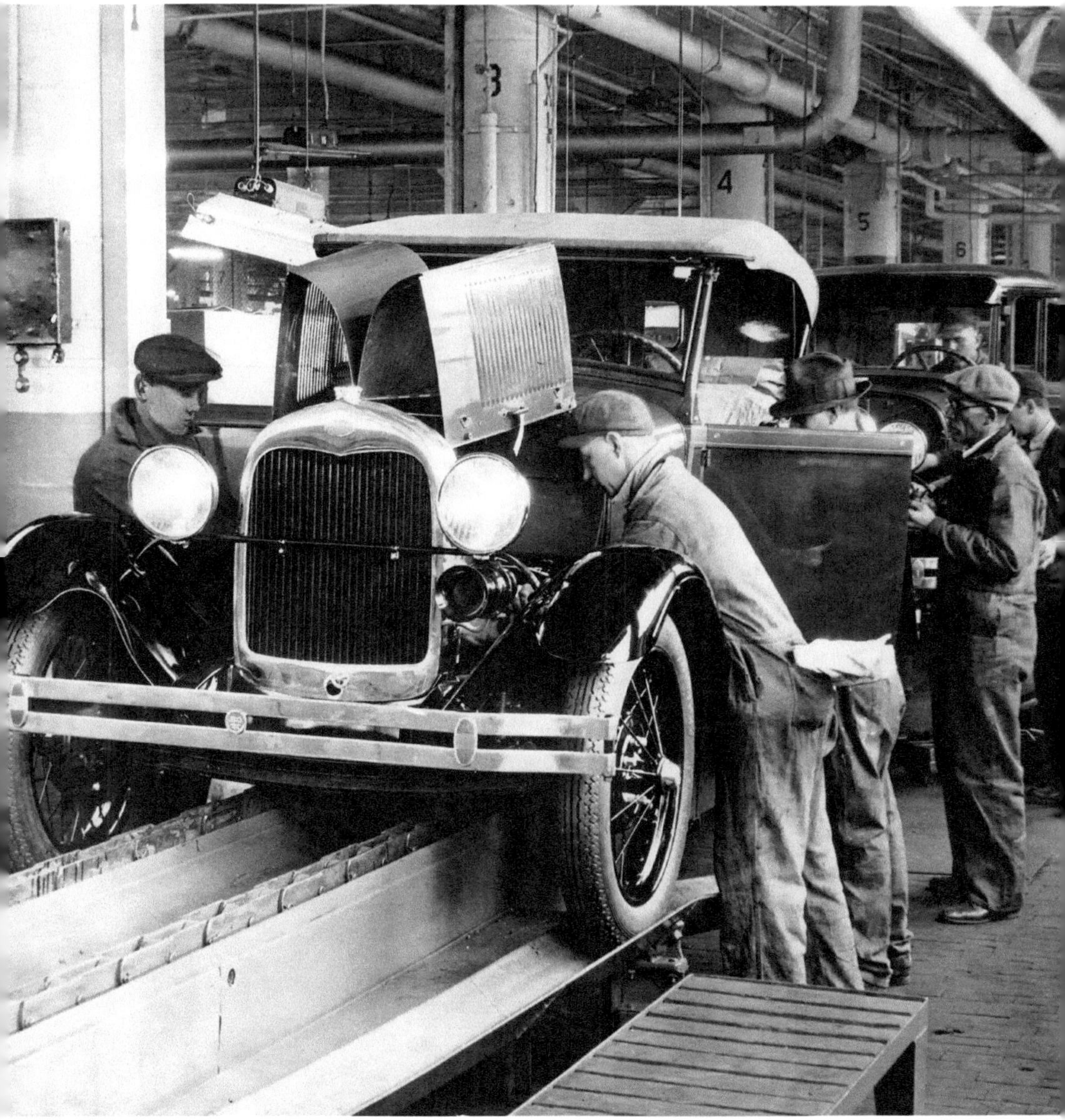

Employees at the Ford Motor Company factory in Dearborn, Michigan, worked together on assembly lines to put together automobiles.

A breakdown on any part of the assembly line means that they all must knack off. The moment this happens, the time is recorded and the worker's pay stops ...

Frequently production reaches a point where it is necessary to shut down early in the day. Very often this breaking-point is at noon. But the men are never advised of this until after they have bought and eaten their lunch at the Ford restaurant. Then they are dismissed for the day, their pay covering only those hours which they have worked ...

The men are given a half-hour for lunch. They are paid twice a month—during their lunch hour. On pay days they must stand in line during this period eating their food. Those who are still in line when the 12:30 gong sounds must come back after work that night and stand in line again ...

—From Carl M. Mydans, "Why Ford Workers Strike," *Nation*, October 25, 1933.

CONSIDER THIS

1. What are some of the things the workers are frustrated about?
2. Why do you think the owner paid the workers on their lunch break?

The Terrifying Reality of Financial Insecurity

Despite how terrible work conditions were, people were still desperate just to have jobs. Workers felt a sense of personal defeat when they were thrown out of their jobs. Unemployed mothers and fathers tried desperately to keep their children housed, clothed, and fed. Men and women wore out their shoes walking the city streets searching for work. Those who were lucky to have jobs may have earned enough to get by but not enough to save. They also feared that any complaint might mean the loss of their job to someone hungrier or more desperate than they were. People were terrified of falling into debt because they were afraid they might never be able to get out.

This family left South Dakota for California in the aftermath of the Dust Bowl. The photo was taken by Dorothea Lange, who is known for the powerful photos she took for the Farm Security Administration.

6 *Depression Narratives*

During the Great Depression, the federal government funded many artists, writers, and photographers through a series of different programs like the Federal Writers' Project and the Farm Security Administration.

Immortalizing the Dust Bowl

For instance, photographer Dorothea Lange worked with the Farm Security Administration, an organization focused on rehabilitating farm areas. Decades of overgrazing, or the overuse of land for feeding livestock, and poor farming methods had left the land vulnerable to wind and weather. These conditions were made worse by a long and terrible drought. It was a prescription for disaster.

The drought began in 1931 and lasted for seven years. In November 1933, one of the first major storms struck. Beginning in South Dakota, the great black dust storm blew long and hard. The winds caused the most damage in the southern Great Plains, which came to be called the Dust Bowl. The states hardest hit were Colorado, Kansas, New Mexico, Oklahoma, and Texas, while bordering states also suffered.

When the wind died down, the farmland that was once planted with wheat was covered by mounds of sand. Farmhouses, barns, and machinery were coated with it. The dust storms continued into 1938. Unable to work the land, farmers and their families packed their belongings into their cars and trucks, abandoned their farms, and headed west to California for what they hoped would be a better life. They were the refugees from the Dust Bowl whom Dorothea Lange photographed and John Steinbeck immortalized, or made famous forever, in his novel *The Grapes of Wrath*.

The Federal Writers

The Federal Writers' Project, part of the WPA, created one of the most lasting book series ever published with government funding. Writers working for the project wrote the American Guide Series, in which each state in the country is covered in detail. Some of these guides can still be found in local libraries. The following selection is taken from *Minnesota: A Guide to the State* and describes the Twin Cities—Minneapolis and Saint Paul. The guide was written in 1938.

> Nucleus of the Northwest, in the hub of an area where 900,000 people live, the Twin Cities, Minneapolis and St. Paul, are at the head of navigation on the Mississippi River—1,596 miles [2,569 km] from where it pours into the Gulf of Mexico—and near the geographical center of North America. Following the river, Minneapolis lies 15 miles [24 km] upstream

from St. Paul, but a crow flying from city hall to city hall would find them only 10 miles [16 km] apart. Together, they form one metropolitan trade center, which ranks eighth in the United States.

To a stranger they seem already to have merged. Connected by a common zone, each has grown up on both sides of the river, their residences intermingled; to the north only a surveyor's line divides them, farther south the mythical "center" of the river marks the boundary. But their citizens know that ... each [city] maintains ... a personality differing sharply from that of its twin.

Even the casual visitor (when he overcomes his bewilderment and determines into which city he has wandered), cannot fail to note certain obvious differences. The St. Paul skyline is all of a piece, Minneapolis sprawls; St. Paul is hilly, Minneapolis is level ... St. Paul's loop streets are narrow and concentrated, while in its twin city the center of activity extends many blocks along the broad shopping avenues ... St. Paul has already attained a degree of mellowness and seems to be clinging to its Victorian dignity, while in Minneapolis dignity is less prized than modern spruceness. The visitor from the East will perhaps feel more at home in St. Paul; if from the West he is likely to prefer Minneapolis.

—From *Minnesota: A Guide to the State* (New York: The Viking Press, 1938).

KEY TERMS AND CONCEPTS

From *Minnesota: A Guide to the State*:
bewilderment A state of confusion.
intermingle To mix together.
nucleus A central or important point.
spruceness A neatness of appearance.
Victorian A style of architecture popular in the nineteenth century. Also refers to a high moral character or prudishness.

From Russell Baker's memoir:
cellophane Transparent wrapping material.

CONSIDER THIS

1. Why do you think the federal government wanted a series of books about the states?
2. What were some of the differences between the Twin Cities in 1938?

Relief for Russell Baker's Family

In 1982, the Virginia-born journalist Russell Baker wrote a memoir about his experiences growing up during the 1930s. After his father's death in 1930, Baker's mother moved her small family first to Belleville, New Jersey, and then to Baltimore, Maryland. During this time, Baker lived with relatives and delivered newspapers while his mother sold magazine subscriptions door-to-door. Together, they experienced the struggle of trying to stay alive. A selection from his book *Growing Up* follows.

> One Saturday morning she told me she'd need Doris [Russell's sister] and me to go with her to pick up some food. I had a small wagon … , and she said I'd better bring it …
>
> "This is where we go," she said … It looked like a grocery … , but it wasn't …
>
> "Are we going on relief?" I asked …
>
> "Don't ask questions …," she said. "Bring that wagon inside."
>
> I did, and watched with a mixture of shame and greed while men filled it with food … There were huge cans of grapefruit juice, big paper sacks of cornmeal, cellophane bags of rice and prunes. It was hard to believe all this was ours for no money at all …
>
> Being on relief was a shameful thing. People who accepted the government's handouts were … people beyond hope. Now we were as low as they were.
>
> —From Russell Baker, *Growing Up* (New York: Congdon & Weed, 1982).

CONSIDER THIS

1. Do you think it is important to have these types of relief programs that provide food to families in need? Why or why not?
2. Do you think Baker ever stopped feeling embarrassed about accepting relief?

Henry J. Antupitsky's Short Story

DeWitt Clinton High School in the Bronx, part of New York City, was an all-boys' school famous for its academic excellence. Famous graduates include writer James Baldwin, photographer Richard Avedon, and screenwriter Paddy Chayefsky. The school's literary magazine, the *Magpie*, contained short stories, poems, drawings, and photographs from the student body. One short story, "Collector's Job" by Henry J. Antupitsky, is included here. In it, the young writer imagines a day in the life of a man employed as a debt collector for a school.

> The brown door opened up its gaping jaws and yawned at him. He rang the bell and took out his slips.
>
> "Collector, madam."
>
> Thick lips and small eyes leered at him.
>
> "No money. My husband is out of work for months. We ..."
>
> He interrupted her wearily.

"But we cannot support your child, madam. Our ... situation demands that you pay or that your child leaves school."

She was going to cry. He saw the tears welling in her eyes. He hated people who wept. He himself had wept too much in the last few weeks before he got his job.

"You will get a call from the central office, madam. Good day."

He walked down the three flights of stairs. In the street, the hush of the night was disturbed rhythmically at even intervals by passing trains. The trolley cars and autos as they passed repeated in a weird metre:

"Out of a job. My husband is not working. I can't pay."

The big blotch of filthy water he passed seemed to be the woman's tears throwing themselves into his face. He closed his eyes trying to shut it all out of his mind. He looked at the slip in his hand. The next one was ten blocks up ... He was working only two hours ... That meant eighty cents. How would he exist? He was making only a dollar a day ... about five dollars a week. He shook his head in despair and tramped wearily up the reeking street.

He braced himself and rang the bell.

"Collector, madam."

And again there followed the usual procedure of talk ... again that ill luck.

"My husband is out of work. We can't pay."

Again he told them of the school's sorely tried finances. He felt the words still ringing in his ears.

"Can't pay. Husband out of work."

Wearily, he walked on.

He searched the letterbox for the name. It was so dark; why couldn't they have a light there? There was a growing pain in his legs and a whirling sound in his head ... He peered intently into the dark, rang the first bell within his reach, and entered the hall.

As he climbed the four stories, he held on to the railing. The ... odor of fried fish met his hungry nostrils and he began to be aware of a gnawing emptiness in his stomach ... He rang the bell.

"Collector, madam."

A small, eager face met his eyes.

"Come right in, please."

She led him into a dungeon reeking with poverty and need.

"Sit down, please."

He declined, afraid that if he sat down, he would never be able to get up.

"Have you change?"

He shook his head ruefully as she went out and he gazed longingly at the chair and the set table.

On her return, he gave her a receipt and left. Again he was ringing the bell. And again the black obscurity of the door opened up to him ...

"Collector, madam."

A pair of beady black eyes met his tired ones angrily.

"So ... what do they want money for? The bills they send me. You tell them at the office that ..."

Her voice became dull and monotonous ... mixed and jumbled. Her face and lips were whirling around him in crazy circles. He closed his eyes for a moment ... sighed, and sank to the ground ...

Dr. Cohen was speaking to his assistant, an intern interested in psychology.

"Exhaustion, hunger, and the continuous repetition of a certain phrase which kept hammering itself ... on his brain. He needs rest and quiet."

The intern, puffed up with his knowledge ... turned to Dr. Cohen.

"That has a technical term. It is called ..."

Dr. Cohen motioned him to be quiet as the phone rang. It was his wife.

There was a collector there.

"Strange," said he, "we have one here, too."

"But he wants money."

"Money? Tell him we can't pay. I am out of work," and with this he hung up.

—From Henry J. Antupitsky, "Collector's Job," in the *Magpie*, June 1932, Vol. 33, No. 2.

CONSIDER THIS

1. Why do you think the main character of this story took on the job of debt collector?
2. Does the ending come as a surprise? Why or why not?

An Entry from Harold L. Ickes's Diary

Harold Ickes was secretary of the interior, or the person responsible for the preservation of federal land, during the presidency of Franklin Roosevelt. Born in Pennsylvania in 1874, Ickes left home at the age of sixteen and moved to Chicago. Upon graduating from the University of Chicago, Ickes worked as a reporter for various newspapers in the city, studied the law, and eventually became a lawyer.

KEY TERMS AND CONCEPTS

From Henry J. Antupitsky's story:

leer To look at someone in an unpleasant way.

metre Meter; rhythm or pace.

monotonous Flat in tone.

obscurity The state of being unknown.

ruefully Sorrowfully.

wearily Tiredly.

From Harold Ickes's diary:

his car Since FDR did not have use of his legs, his car was fitted with hand controls for the gas and brake.

jolly Happy.

ravine A deep, narrow valley with steep sides.

Secret Service The security team that protects the president.

He became part of FDR's cabinet in 1933 and held his post until 1946. Harold Ickes kept a diary of the first thousand days of the Roosevelt administration and wrote the following description of the president at Warm Springs, Georgia. FDR, who had polio, often visited this thermal spring and its treatment center, which he built to help other victims of the disease. The following is an entry from November 1933.

> I took the train for Atlanta, Georgia ... Colonel McIntyre ... drove me over to Warm Springs, where I was the personal guest of the President. He has a

Harold L. Ickes was one of the longest-serving cabinet members in US history. His son Harold M. Ickes went on to serve as one of the top aides in President Bill Clinton's administration.

small cottage ... located on the edge of a well-wooded ravine ... The President is always charming but he was delightful at Warm Springs. Everyone there loves him, and crowds hang outside the gate ... just to see him and cheer him ... Some of the surrounding country is very lovely, and while I was there he took me driving on two or three occasions. He goes anywhere in his car, right into the woods, taking a real delight in making it difficult for the Secret Service car to follow him. I have never had contact with a man who was loved as he is. To the people of Warm Springs he is just a big jolly brother.

—From *The Secret Diary of Harold L. Ickes, The First Thousand Days, 1933–1936* (New York: Simon & Schuster, 1953).

CONSIDER THIS

1. What aspect of FDR's personality impressed Ickes?
2. Why do you think the people of Warm Springs were particularly fond of FDR?

The End and the Beginning

Roosevelt was responsible for the New Deal programs that helped pull people in the country out of financial hardship. For the first time, the government took responsibility for providing every American with a security net. Even though the Depression came to an end as the United States began to produce materials needed for World War II, the programs started during this decade of financial crisis would change the United States forever.

During World War II, Schick Inc., a company known for manufacturing electric dry shavers, allowed its Stamford, Connecticut, plant to be used for war production. For instance, the company made stadimeters, devices used to measure the distance of an object, for the US Navy.

7 *Life-Changing and Long-Lasting Effects*

The effects of the Great Depression and the New Deal's response to it were felt in ways large and small across the United States. Workers gained access to old-age pensions, the guarantee of a minimum wage, and limits on how many hours they could be asked to work. The desperate poor were given relief payments. Farmers gained government assistance in improving agricultural methods and for dealing with an excess of crops. The nation's system of roads, bridges, and parks was improved with government funding and work programs. Additionally, an entire region experienced economic development and modernization as a result of a massive government program of dam building and electrification.

A New Attitude

As the New Deal passed into history, American attitudes about government's role—especially the federal government's role—in their lives changed. The idea that government had a responsibility to care for the neediest of its citizens began to take hold. While many Americans prided themselves on their self-sufficiency and ability to survive tough times, many more came to believe that only the federal government could provide real help for certain basic problems.

The Social Security Act

Only a few states had social security laws in 1929. Social security is any system that provides financial support to people who do not have income. However, the federal government did not create a system of national social security until 1935, when Congress passed the Social Security Act.

The core of the Social Security program was the old-age pension. This was a benefit paid to people over the age of sixty-five. The amount each individual would receive would be based on their prior earnings. The money to pay for the pensions was accumulated from taxes taken out of employees' paychecks and employers' payrolls, with the tax rate increasing over the years. An additional fund was set up for future generations. The Social Security Act also provided for federal money to help states aid the disabled, needy children, the old, and the poor. The Social Security Administration, set up by the act, is still in existence today. The following are excerpts from the original Social Security Act.

> SECTION 1 For the purpose of enabling each State to furnish financial assistance ... to aged needy

individuals, there is hereby authorized ... the sum of $49,750,000 and there is hereby authorized to be appropriated for each fiscal year thereafter a sum sufficient to carry out the purposes of this title.

SECTION 201 There is hereby created an account in the Treasury of the United States to be known as the "Old-Age Reserve Account."

SECTION 202 Every qualified individual shall be entitled to receive ... beginning on the date he attains the age of sixty-five ... an old-age benefit.

SECTION 401 For the purpose of enabling each State to furnish financial assistance, as far as practicable under the conditions in such State, to needy dependent children, there is hereby authorized to be appropriated ... the sum of $24,750,000 ... to carry out the purpose of this title.

—From Henry Steele Commager, ed., "U.S. Statutes at Large," in *Documents of American History*, Vol. XLIX (New York: Appleton-Century-Crofts, 1963).

CONSIDER THIS

1. In addition to older Americans, who else is eligible to collect social security?
2. In your opinion, should social security be continued? Why or why not?

KEY TERMS AND CONCEPTS

From the Social Security Act:

attain To achieve.

fiscal year A year as considered for tax or accounting purposes. It's not necessarily the same as a calendar year, which stretches from January 1 to December 31.

From Rose Dudley Scearce's account:

Aladdin lamp An oil or kerosene lamp.

humor Mood.

I.E.S. The Illuminating Engineering Society was a society created to educate people about proper lighting.

pike A road.

range A stove.

Rural Electrification Administration: Let There Be Light

In the early 1930s, many rural areas of the United States—especially in the South—still had no electricity. By 1939, things had changed dramatically. The Rural Electrification Administration (REA), created in 1935, connected farmhouses to poles carrying electric lines. It also helped set up rural electric cooperatives, or organizations that are owned and run by their members. Members bought their electricity from the cooperative. With access to electricity, farmers and others began to electrify their houses and introduce labor-saving devices. In the following document, a farm woman in Kentucky describes how the introduction of electricity has changed her life.

> The first benefit we received from the REA service was lights ... My little boy expressed my sentiments when he said, "Mother, I didn't realize how dark our house was until we got electric lights." We had been reading by an Aladdin lamp and thought it was good, but it didn't compare with our I.E.S. reading lamp.
>
> Recently, I read in the *Rural Electrification News* that the radio was the most popular appliance that had been bought. So, like the rest of the people, we changed our storage-battery radio into an electric radio. This was our next benefit.
>
> Next we bought an electric refrigerator ... The next benefit we received from the current was our electric stove.

This Rural Electrification Administration advertisement boasts the comfort electricity can bring to one's life.

We were so anxious for the current that we wired our house many months before the current was turned on, and we wired our kitchen for an electric range.

Before the current was turned on, when anyone asked me what appliance I wanted most I always said that I wanted a vacuum cleaner ... I have an old-fashioned Brussells body carpet on my living-room floor, and when I swept it I raised as much dust as if I had been sweeping the dusty pike. When I finished I was choking with the dust, the carpet was not clean, and I was in a bad humor. Now with the vacuum cleaner, I can even dust the furniture before I clean the carpet, the carpet gets clean, and I stay in a good humor.

So you see I am thoroughly enjoying the many things that electricity had made possible, and I am enjoying life more.

—From Rose Dudley Scearce, Member, Shelby (Ky.) Rural Electric Cooperative, "What REA Service Means to Our Farm Home."

CONSIDER THIS

1. How did people read before electric lighting became available?
2. How would your life be different if you had no electricity?

Changes in the Workplace

Labor unions saw the economic crisis of the Great Depression as an opportunity to improve the life of the American worker. Across the nation, they struggled to organize workers into unions that would—through strikes and collective bargaining—force employers to improve wages and working conditions. Often companies would hire "scabs," or people who would work despite the strike, to replace the workers who had gone out on strike. Sometimes violence would erupt between the two groups.

As a result, workers developed a new tactic: the sit-down strike. One of the most famous sit-down strikes of the Depression era took place between 1936 and 1937, against General Motors in Flint, Michigan, by the United Auto Workers. The strike lasted forty-four days and was considered a major victory for Flint's auto workers and for the labor movement in general.

Even though some workers fought for their rights, others ended up losing their jobs. Some workers during the Great Depression lost their jobs, and their self-respect, because of changes in technology, an ongoing process of the Industrial Revolution. When a new, highly mechanized steel mill went up in one town in Pennsylvania, 1,300 of the 1,500 steelworkers in the town were replaced by machines. In the following account, we hear the voice of a highly skilled "old hand" mourning the loss of his craft.

> Just before leaving the [new] mill I met Mike Michaels, an officer of the local union, sweeping up paper, bale tie ends, and dust in the shipping room. Mike came to America from Wales in 1904 at the age of fifteen. His father was one of the experienced Welsh hand-mill workers the company imported to run the now abandoned sheet mill when it was first built. Mike had worked there himself for over thirty

years until it was closed last year. For twenty years he was a roller, an "aristocrat of labor," earning $12 to $15 a day. Now he was doing a laborer's job, at 63 cents an hour. Less than two hundred of the fifteen hundred displaced sheet mill workers in Steelville found jobs in the strip mill. "What do you think of her?" Mike asked.

"It's impressive," a friend with me replied, "impressive—all that big automatic machinery running virtually without manpower ..." Mike leaned on his broom and with some bitterness said: "Impressive, huh! I'd call it oppressive, I would. Here I am pushing a broom, where I started over thirty years back. I'm not an old man yet. I've not turned fifty. But I'm too old to work on any of that impressive, I call it oppressive, machinery. They got a bunch of button pushers running this mill, young palookas, I call them, just kids."

Mike pointed to the endless ceiling with massive machinery under it. "Look at her!" he said. "You know what we call her?—'The Big Morgue.' The few of us old hand-mill men that got something to do here ain't so bad off as the thirteen hundred or more fellows that are out starving on relief or struggling on WPA. When we meet on the street and get to talkin we call this 'the big Morgue,' the place where all our jobs went dead."

—From Harold J. Ruttenberg, "The Big Morgue," in *Survey Graphic*, April 1939.

KEY TERMS AND CONCEPTS

From the Pennsylvania steel mill account:

"aristocrat of labor" Someone with a high-paying position.

bale tie Wires for tying up bundles.

palooka A stupid or not well-mannered person.

roller A person who worked the rolling mill, which was used to make metal thinner or more uniform in texture and shape.

CONSIDER THIS

1. What happened to the worker described in this article?
2. Why was he called an "aristocrat of labor"?
3. Can you think of jobs in other industries that have been lost to machines since the Great Depression?

A Good Effort

While it was true that many people went without food, housing, and jobs during the 1930s, some families managed to find enough work and get enough food to keep their lives intact. Ultimately, the United States was able to survive the Great Depression, but it wasn't necessarily Roosevelt or the New Deal that fixed the problem.

The programs Roosevelt put into action helped relieve some of the crisis. However, his programs weren't entirely a success.

More than anything, Roosevelt renewed people's faith in the US democracy at a time when people greatly feared communism and fascism, an extreme system of government and social organization, which was emerging in Europe.

Unfortunately, the New Deal and Roosevelt's efforts didn't actually pull the United States out of the Depression. In fact, in 1937, there was another dip in the economy that reminded people of the crash in 1929. Emergency funds were again used to help bolster businesses, but unemployment and poverty continued to grow. Things finally started to change, however, when war was on the horizon.

World War II

On September 1, 1939, Adolf Hitler, who ruled Germany as a dictator, or someone with complete power, invaded Poland. Within a few days, World War II had officially started. It was a war that involved Germany, Italy, and Japan on one side and France, Great Britain, the United States, and the Soviet Union on the other. In many ways, the war was a continuation of World War I.

Isolationism

Before the United States officially joined the war in December 1941, many Americans were hesitant about the idea of getting involved in international affairs. Many of them felt that US involvement in World War I had been a mistake and wanted to stay out of this new conflict.

The United States found itself in a period of isolationism, or a time when a country is only interested in its own politics and affairs. Only after certain turns in the early war, like the fall of France to Germany, did Roosevelt and Congress send resources to Great Britain. Despite public opinions that supported Britain, many Americans continued to want to stay out of the war.

During the attack on Pearl Harbor, crew members of the USS *California* were forced to abandon the ship after being hit by several bombs and torpedoes. Over one hundred of its crew members died.

This, in many ways, made sense, as the country was barely recovering from years of financial crisis.

Still, Roosevelt found ways to support the British by sending aid in the form of supplies. These supplies had to be created somewhere. The war abroad thus provided new manufacturing opportunities for people in the United States, who scrambled to produce goods and weapons.

US Involvement in World War II

Despite resistance to the war, the United States eventually officially joined the effort after the Japanese attacked Pearl Harbor, a naval base in Hawaii, on December 7, 1941. The attack killed nearly 2,500 people and left more than 1,000 injured. As the United States joined the war effort, war production increased. By 1944, war production in the United States was more than twice the production by all of the enemy countries combined. This increase in production meant that many Americans found themselves with full-time employment again.

In the shadow of the war, the Great Depression came to a close.

The Era's Legacy

Today, Americans still enjoy many of the facilities created during the Great Depression. Many museums, national parks, and highways were created by people working as part of the New Deal programs. Similarly, some of the public aid organizations, like the Social Security Administration and the Tennessee Valley Authority, come from Depression-era legislation. People also carry with them lessons learned from the Depression.

In 2008, the United States faced the greatest financial hardships since the Depression. Again, this was a time period in which everyone, not just the United States, felt the effects of a financial crisis. Similarly, the recession started when prices, of houses this time, seemed to soar. A sudden downturn led to a crisis for banks and insurance companies. Additionally, the American automobile industry took a hit. Banks began to fear that people and companies would not be able to pay them back and stopped making loans that many people and businesses needed.

Again, the government, this time run by President Barack Obama, set out to fix the economy. Although the economy and stock market recovered somewhat by the end of 2009, the damage had been done. People found themselves unemployed and without homes for several of the following years.

As with the Great Depression, people had to try to rebuild their lives both with the help of the government and the courage to keep pressing forward in the face of hardship.

CHRONOLOGY

1914 World War I begins.

1918 World War I ends.

1929 The stock market crash wipes out billions of dollars in investments.

1930 President Hoover asks Congress for millions of dollars to support public works. The number of unemployed reaches 4.5 million. Over one thousand banks fail, including the Bank of the United States in New York City.

1931 A seven-year drought begins in the southern Great Plains.

1932 The Reconstruction Finance Corporation is established to help the nation's banks, insurance companies, and railroads; it is later expanded to aid agricultural credit groups and to fund public works. The Bonus Army marches to Washington, DC, to demand their bonuses, and violence erupts. Franklin Delano Roosevelt is elected president.

1933 Governor of Michigan declares a one-day bank holiday; other governors follow and begin to close banks in their states to keep panic-stricken depositors from withdrawing money. Approximately fifteen million Americans are unemployed. FDR declares a four-day national bank holiday as one of his first acts as president. He launches the first round of New Deal legislation, which establishes the Civilian Conservation Corps, the Public Works Administration, and the National Recovery Administration.

1934 Dust storms spread over the southern plains and southwest, destroying millions of acres of farmland and forcing thousands of people to leave their homes. Huey Long launches his "Share Our Wealth" program. The Securities and Exchange Commission is established to regulate stock exchanges and the trading of stocks.

1935 The Works Progress Administration, later known as the Work Projects Administration, is established. The Social Security Act is passed, creating financial assistance programs. The Rural Electrification Administration, responsible for providing electricity to people in remote or rural areas, is established. The National Labor Relations Board, to protect workers' rights, is established.

1936 President Roosevelt is elected for a second term.

1937 A recession hits the country.

1938 A US minimum wage is set.

1939 World War II begins when Germany invades Poland. The Depression in the United States begins to ease as factories gear up to produce war supplies for nations at war with Germany.

GLOSSARY

assets Items of ownership that can be converted into cash; also, the total resources of a person or business.

bankrupt Legally declared to be unable to pay one's debts.

bolster To support or strengthen something.

capital Wealth, in the form of money or property, owned or used by an individual or business.

communism A political system in which the government, as opposed to private businesses, owns everything and resources are shared with each individual based on merit and need. It is the opposite of the US system, which is based on a capitalist democracy, where the government has less control and people and private businesses are more in control.

conserve To protect and maintain, particularly natural landscapes, from harm.

economy The way a nation's goods and services are produced, distributed, and used.

Great Depression A prolonged period from 1929 to 1939 during which employment, values of stock, and businesses declined or suffered because of an economic downturn.

investor A person who puts money into the stock market in hopes of making money.

labor union An organization of workers formed to protect their rights and interests at a company.

legislation A law.

overspeculation The assumption that stocks will make more of a profit than they actually can.

persist To continue in the face of difficulty or opposition.

relief Money, food, and clothing given by the government to those in need during the Great Depression.

share Ownership of one of the equal parts of a company's capital, or money; people who own shares in a company have a right to a portion of the company's profits.

social security A government program of guaranteed payments to the elderly, the unemployed, and the disabled made possible by a system of payroll deductions.

stock A share of ownership in a business or corporation.

strike A work stoppage carried out by employees against an employer with the aim of forcing the employer to pay higher wages, improve working conditions, or shorten work hours.

underconsumption An economic condition in which people, because of lack of money or confidence, buy less than what is readily available from a business, thus causing the business to fail.

welfare Government help given to those in need until they are able to take care of themselves.

FURTHER INFORMATION

Books

Hurt, Avery Elizabeth. *The Great Depression.* The Interwar Years. New York: Cavendish Square Publishing, 2017.

Hyde, Natalie. *Black Tuesday and the Great Depression.* Uncovering the Past: Analyzing Primary Sources. New York: Crabtree Publishing Company, 2015.

Nardo, Don. *The Presidency of Franklin D. Roosevelt: Confronting the Great Depression and World War II.* The Greatest US Presidents. North Mankato, MN: Compass Point Books, 2014.

Saidian, Siyavush. *The Great Depression: Worldwide Economic Crisis.* American History. New York: Lucent Books, 2017.

Websites

Digital History: Great Depression

http://www.digitalhistory.uh.edu/era.cfm?eraID=14&smtID=1

This website offers an overview of the Great Depression, including primary-source documents, music, film, and photographs.

A New Deal for the Arts

https://www.archives.gov/exhibits/new_deal_for_the_arts/index.html

Between 1933 and 1943, the federal government financially supported artists, writers, and performers. This website features some of the art that came out of this era.

Social Welfare History Project

https://socialwelfare.library.vcu.edu

This awareness-based project founded by Dr. John E. Hasan provides people with information about the long and complicated history of social reform, or societal changes, and welfare services, like those created by Roosevelt during the Depression. It provides primary sources related to reform and welfare from the colonial era to the present day.

Videos

America in Color: The 1920s

https://www.youtube.com/watch?v=G7-uIKyavxE

This Smithsonian video features footage from the Roaring Twenties, the decade before the Great Depression hit. It discusses what led to the Great Depression.

America, the Story of Us: FDR

https://www.youtube.com/watch?v=O8uaD_Ob21I

This brief video provides an overview of FDR's impact on the American people during the Great Depression.

Organizations

Arthurdale Heritage: New Deal Homestead Museum
PO Box 850
Arthurdale, WV 26520
(304) 864-3959
Website: https://arthurdaleheritage.org

Arthurdale is a preserved New Deal homestead town. In this town, the federal government gave families land, homes, food, and livestock. This museum tells their stories and the story of First Lady Eleanor Roosevelt's commitment to the community.

Franklin Delano Roosevelt Presidential Library and Museum
4079 Albany Post Road
Hyde Park, NY 12538
(845) 486-7770
Website: https://fdrlibrary.org

This library and museum features collections of letters, photographs, books, periodicals, and more related to Franklin Delano Roosevelt, his family, and his political career.

Herbert Hoover Presidential Library and Museum
210 Parkside Drive
West Branch, IA 52358
(319) 643-5301
Website: https://hoover.archives.gov

Opened August 1962, the Hoover Library and Museum features archives related to Hoover's long career of public service, including the time he served as president during the Great Depression.

Lakeshore Museum Center:
Scolnik House of the Depression Era
504 W. Clay Avenue
Muskegon, MI 49440
(231) 722-7578
Website: https://www.lakeshoremuseum.org/project/scolnik-house-of-the-depression-era

In the Scolnik House, which tells the story of Depression-era families in Michigan, visitors can "try on period clothing, help do laundry, and explore the garden" to get a better understanding of life during the Depression.

The Living New Deal
Department of Geography
505 McCone Hall
University of California
Berkeley, CA 94720
(510) 642-5987
Website: https://livingnewdeal.org

This nonprofit organization strives to document the legacy of the variety of New Deal public works projects through maps and research.

Tennessee Valley Authority
400 West Summit Hill Drive
Knoxville, TN 37902
(865) 632-2101
Website: https://www.tva.gov

This alphabet soup organization was established in 1933 as part of President Roosevelt's New Deal legislation to bring electricity and flood control to the Tennessee River basin. Today, it continues that work.

INDEX

Page numbers in **boldface** refer to images.

ABOUT THE AUTHORS

Chet'la Sebree is a writer, editor, and researcher from the Mid-Atlantic. She has received degrees in English and writing from the University of Richmond and American University. She has worked on several books about US history, including the Courting History series for Cavendish Square Publishing. Her research focus is early American history.

Adriane Ruggiero writes and edits nonfiction works with an emphasis on history and international affairs. She holds a master's degree in history and education and a bachelor's degree in history. Ruggiero has published works about the United States' involvement in both World Wars and has edited a series on immigration to the United States, among many others. Additionally, she has served as a contributor to major reference texts such as *The Dictionary of the Middle Ages*, *The Encyclopedia of Ancient Greece and Rome*, and *Magill's Encyclopedia of Military History*.